I0815422

The Bible, Simplified

The Bible, Simplified

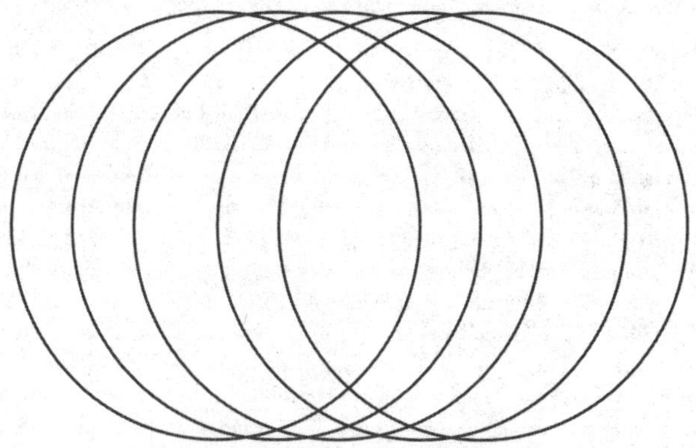

Learn the Story, Live the Story

Zach Windahl

An Imprint of Thomas Nelson

The Bible, Simplified

Published in Nashville, Tennessee, by Nelson Books, an imprint of Thomas Nelson. Nelson Books and Thomas Nelson are registered trademarks of HarperCollins Christian Publishing, Inc.

Author is represented by the literary agency of The Fedd Agency, Inc., P. O. Box 341973, Austin, Texas 78734.

Thomas Nelson titles may be purchased in bulk for educational, business, fundraising, or sales promotional use. For information, please email SpecialMarkets@ThomasNelson.com.

Library of Congress Cataloging-in-Publication Data

Names: Windahl, Zach author
Title: The Bible, simplified : learn the story, live the story / Zach Windahl.
Description: Nashville, Tennessee : Nelson Books, [2025] | Includes bibliographical references. | Summary: "You don't need a theology degree to understand the Bible--you just need 60 days. Join bestselling author Zach Windahl on a journey to a deeper, more meaningful relationship with God through his Word"-- Provided by publisher.
Identifiers: LCCN 2025002614 (print) | LCCN 2025002615 (ebook) | ISBN 9781400252534 hardcover | ISBN 9781400253166 ebook
Subjects: LCSH: Bible--Introductions
Classification: LCC BS475.3 .W545 2025 (print) | LCC BS475.3 (ebook) | DDC 220.6/1--dc23/eng/20250414
LC record available at https://lccn.loc.gov/2025002614
LC ebook record available at https://lccn.loc.gov/2025002615

Printed in the United States of America

25 26 27 28 29 LBC 8 7 6 5 4

To my firstborn son, Eben.

May your life become a reflection of Jesus.

Contents

Introduction

Raise your hand if you grew up going to church but still don't know the Bible.

Or what if you're a new Christian but don't know where to begin?

Or what if you're just curious about Jesus and figured the Bible is the best place to learn about him?

I was in that same spot for years. Even though I went to church every week for most of my life, my relationship with the Bible wasn't there at all. I mean, have you ever opened the Bible with no understanding of the text? It's hundreds of thin pages full of stories that leave you more confused than you were before you opened it.

But as a Christian, you're supposed to fall in love with this stuff. How is that even possible?

The first half is confusing, aside from the stories we learn about in Sunday school, which are far more disturbing when you read them as an adult. Then Jesus comes and he seems cool, but you aren't really sure why he had to die for you. Then the last pages are scary because they talk about the end of the world and a dragon.

It's overwhelming.

It's intimidating.

You don't know where to start.

I get it. Many of us have been there. It's far easier to just go to church on Sunday and be inspired by your pastor than to put in the work yourself—but that leaves you missing out on so much.

You don't want to be like that anymore. That's where this book comes in. You're taking a step in the other direction, and we're going to learn the Bible together. God has given us the Bible as a how-to guide for making the most out of life.

A. W. Tozer once said, "The Word of God well understood and religiously obeyed is the shortest route to spiritual perfection. And we must not select a few favorite passages to the exclusion of others. Nothing less than a whole Bible can make a whole Christian."[1]

The Bible should be our lifeline. We need to study it as if we need it to breathe.

The Bible, Simplified will help you grow in your faith.

In this book, I've simplified the story of the Bible into forty short chapters. Each one explores a different part of the book, from the origins of the universe and Israel's journey out of slavery, to the teachings of Jesus and his vision for a new world that is to come. Each topic is broken down into bite-sized chunks to keep you on track through the whole Bible, to help you understand how the entire story plays into God's big plan. My goal is to make the Bible approachable, so you can become confident in your understanding of it and see its relevance to your life.

While information about the Bible matters, this book's purpose is to help you transform your life and your relationship with God through the Bible. I want you to understand the Bible for yourself, not be overwhelmed or intimidated by it. Life is already complicated; feeling spiritually disconnected shouldn't add to the weight.

Now, this book is not meant to replace your reading of the actual Bible. The goal is to build your foundation so you fall more and more in love with Scripture from here on out. I know what it's like to read the Bible and have absolutely no idea what is happening. This should solve that problem by giving you context of the entire storyline to prepare you for a lifetime of studying God's Word.

There is an ancient practice for Jewish kids that took place on the first day of school. The rabbi would hand the students slates with the words of the Hebrew alphabet written on them, and as he read the letters, the kids would repeat them back to him. Then the rabbi would cover the slate in honey and have the students lick it clean. The ritual was an illustration of how the words of God are as sweet as honey to the soul.

That may not be how you feel about Scripture right now. But we're going to get there in the next forty chapters.

One more thing: You may be skeptical and thinking to yourself, *Aren't there a ton of different ways to interpret the Bible? How do I know I can trust this guy?*

You're 100 percent correct to be asking these questions! If you read something that doesn't make sense, or if you disagree and want to explore further, I recommend highlighting the passage and going back to see what other people say about it. On my end, I'll do my best to keep my personal opinion out of things and stay right in the middle of the road doctrinally.

My hope is for you to understand the Bible, no matter your church background. This isn't meant to be a commentary, nor is it meant to definitively answer every single question you might have. Rather, I'm discussing the Bible story in a simplified way to inspire you to study it yourself. You will spend the rest of your life building upon this foundation of Scripture.

That's all for now. See you in chapter 1.

Part One

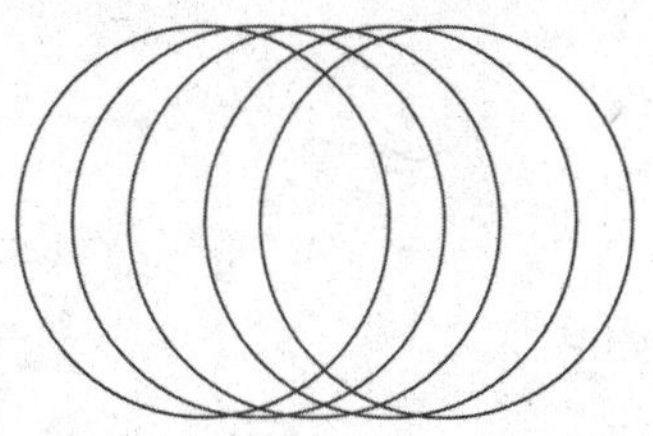

INTRODUCTION TO THE BIBLE

Chapter 1

What Is the Bible?

Have you ever thought about what the Bible actually is?

Or have you just accepted it to be the holy book of Christianity?

If I asked you to tell me the storyline of the Scriptures, could you do it?

Or if I said there were sixty-six books within the Bible, would you know why? Or what they are?

The Bible is complex. It's intricate. It can be confusing if you don't understand its organization or the literary tools its authors used.

But it's the most beautiful literary work the world has ever known.

I call it a "literary work" because the Bible isn't just a single book. It's a collection of books that explores the interactions between God and humanity, laying the groundwork for why we exist as humans and what we are called to be.

The word *Bible* means "book," originally coming from the Greek word *biblia*. Prior to the printing press, the separate books contained within the Bible were written on scrolls. You will notice as we move forward that some of these books are split into two parts (such as 1 Samuel and 2 Samuel, 1 Kings and 2 Kings, etc.). This is because the content was too big to fit onto one scroll, so it was divided between two scrolls, and over the years tradition has kept them separated.

As you flip through the Bible, you will notice two major sections: the Old Testament and the New Testament.

The Old Testament is the story of God building a nation of people called Israel.

The New Testament is the story of God sending his Son, Jesus, as the Savior of the world to be born in that nation.

These stories aren't like just any old history book. They're God's history book. And if you have a relationship with him, you are now part of the family of God.

The story of Abraham is now your story.
The story of the Israelites' exodus out of Egypt is now your story.
The story of how they entered the promised land and fell away from faith is now your story.

When we learn to accept these stories as our own, we can better see how we have been placed within God's story.

Now, our Old Testament contains the same books as the Hebrew Bible. Something many people may not realize is that Jesus was Jewish. Christianity is the simple fact that we believe Jesus to be the long-awaited Messiah of the Jewish faith.

So Christians and Jewish people share a common history.

The Old Testament is a collection of thirty-nine books written in both Hebrew and Aramaic, exploring topics like the creation of the world, the

Israelites' exodus from Egypt, their journey to the promised land, how they built the kingdom and the temple, and how they lost it all because of disobedience. (We'll explore that more later on.)

The Old Testament can be divided into five major sections:

Torah (the Law or the Pentateuch)	History	Poetry	Major Prophets	Minor Prophets
• Genesis • Exodus • Leviticus • Numbers • Deuteronomy	• Joshua • Judges • Ruth • 1 and 2 Samuel • 1 and 2 Kings • 1 and 2 Chronicles • Ezra • Nehemiah • Esther	• Job • Psalms • Proverbs • Ecclesiastes • Song of Songs	• Isaiah • Jeremiah • Lamentations • Ezekiel • Daniel	• Hosea • Joel • Amos • Obadiah • Jonah • Micah • Nahum • Habakkuk • Zephaniah • Haggai • Zechariah • Malachi

Are you following along here?

If not, let me confuse you a little more: The books of the Bible aren't in chronological order. They tell an interwoven story of how God is using a specific group of people to bring his kingdom to the world. That's why it's so helpful to have a little historical context. The Bible isn't the type of book you can read one time and then be good for the rest of your life. No matter how many times you read it, you'll never understand it all.

And that's okay.

The Old Testament ends with a cliff-hanger, anticipating the Messiah's arrival to restore the Jewish people to a "golden era."

And then the story ends.

And the people wait.

As Christians, our story picks up four hundred years after the final Old Testament book was written, when a man arrived in the Galilee region claiming he was the Messiah. His name was Jesus, and we believe he was God in human form, coming to redeem the world, restoring it to God's original plan.

This is where our New Testament comes in, the second major section in Scripture. The New Testament contains twenty-seven books written in Greek, exploring the life, death, and resurrection of Jesus. It also explores the early spread of Christianity and includes a bunch of letters written to different people about how to live as followers of Jesus.

The New Testament can be divided into four main sections:

History	Pauline Epistles	General Epistles	Prophecy
• Matthew • Mark • Luke • John • Acts	• Romans • 1 and 2 Corinthians • Galatians • Ephesians • Philippians • Colossians • 1 and 2 Thessalonians • 1 and 2 Timothy • Titus • Philemon	• Hebrews • James • 1 and 2 Peter • 1, 2, and 3 John • Jude	• Revelation

Understanding that each book of the Bible fits into a specific literary category or genre will impact the way you read the book itself.

For example, you wouldn't approach a mystery novel the same way you would a book of leadership advice. So if you read one of the letters (epistles) the way you read a book of prophecy, you won't make sense of the letter. If you read a historical story the same way you read a book of poetry, it won't make sense either.

Within each genre in the Bible (history, prophecy, epistle, etc.), we find three main literary styles to focus on:

1. **Narrative (or story):** Nearly half of the Bible consists of narrative or story. Why? Because humans gravitate toward a good story. Stories make sense to us. God also loves a good story.
2. **Poetry:** Poetry makes up about one-third of the text. These poems were meant to be sung, prayed, or said aloud in group settings. You've probably heard of the largest book of the Bible that contains poetry: the Psalms. They share God's truth through emotions and images.
3. **Discourse:** *Discourse* is a fancy word for writing that is meant to persuade a person to change their way of thinking or doing. It's more conversational and to the point, presenting an idea. This is what you'll find in a lot of Jesus' sermons and the letters in the New Testament. These are teaching moments.[1]

If we want to grasp what the biblical authors are writing about, we need to understand the style of writing they are using.

Speaking of authors, this is where the Bible gets really interesting, because God didn't write the Bible and drop it from the sky.

The Bible was written by forty different authors
over the span of fifteen hundred years
from three continents
in three languages
all inspired by God.

These authors were farmers and kings and fishermen and prisoners and priests and shepherds and a tax collector and even a doctor. The collection of people is very diverse. Yet when you put all sixty-six books together into one big book, it's perfectly arranged.

Can you imagine forty people from different cultures and languages writing one part of a story over the course of fifteen hundred years and maintaining a consistent storyline, all without ever knowing that their work would one day be compiled? It's a miracle that this story, once it was combined, makes any sense at all.

"Well, wait," you might be asking, "if all these separate books were written so far apart, then who was in charge of putting them all together?"

I'm glad you asked.

What you're asking about is the biblical canon, or the canon of Scripture. The word *canon* refers to the standard that we hold something to or the authority we give it. In this case, we hold Scripture to the highest standard and authority possible. So the biblical canon is the compilation of all the books that meet that extraordinary standard.

The Hebrew Bible's compilation period began during the return from Babylonian exile (which we'll talk about later) in the fifth and sixth centuries BC, with the final book being added to the list during the first century BC.

Because the rabbis took their copying work seriously, not much debate takes place around the Old Testament canon. Remember, no printing presses existed at this time. Every document, scroll, or book in the world was handwritten.

So the rabbis created schools devoted to copying Scripture onto papyrus or leather, word for word, letter by letter. They believed that if they messed up the Word of God, they would be sent back to exile—so they were incredibly meticulous about every line and every dot.

Does that mean no errors were introduced as time passed on? Of course not. Just as you and I mess up words and letters when we write something down, some typos slipped through. But so many early copies of Old Testament Scripture have been found through archaeological digs that we are now able to compare the texts and find the errors.

The largest debate among the early church regarding the Bible concerned which books should be included in the New Testament. The Old Testament was solidified, but with so many letters and stories floating around, the New Testament still had no defined list.

Enter church councils.

The early church was very aware that they were one body, so they could make decisions about which books were recognized as Scripture and which ones were not.

As the councils looked at all the documents circulating at the time, these were the major criteria they considered:

1. Was it written by someone who was a friend of Jesus or at least a friend of a friend?
2. Did it agree with other Scripture that was already considered God-inspired?

If the answer to both questions was yes, the text would be viewed as authoritative. Just as we believe God inspired the hands of the writers, we also believe God inspired the councils as they recognized the canon and what was to be included.

In AD 367, Athanasius, Bishop of Alexandria, named the complete list of our current twenty-seven-book New Testament in its full form for the first time.[2]

This list of twenty-seven books then became the gold standard for what constituted the New Testament. This list was further locked in when Jerome compiled his Latin Vulgate Bible from AD 383 to 404, which then became the main Bible of the West.[3]

In chapter 2 we'll take a practical but deeper look at how to read this canon.

One-Sentence Recap

The Bible is a library of sixty-six books, written by forty different authors, over the span of fifteen hundred years, telling the story of God's relationship with humanity and what our role on earth is.

Chapter 2

How to Read the Bible

Had you never opened a Bible before and I asked you to flip to John 3:16, you would most likely be very confused. You could probably guess that the chapter was called John, but the numbers wouldn't make sense to you at all because most books aren't organized in this way.

Not until AD 1560 with the printing of the Geneva Bible did we see the inclusion of both chapter and verse divisions throughout the entirety of Scripture. And since then, including these divisions has been common practice.

So today, when I ask you to flip your Bible open to John 3:16,

- **John** is the title of the book you look for,
- **3** is the chapter (big number), and
- **16** is the verse (little number at the end of some sentences and phrases).

Once you understand how to read the Bible, how are you supposed to study it?

1. Pray beforehand.
2. Read in context.

First, remind yourself to pray before you open Scripture. The phrase "pray before opening" in all caps is literally written in Sharpie across the first page of my Bible so I don't forget. Prayer is crucial. If you've said yes to Jesus, you have the same Holy Spirit inside you that inspired the Bible's original authors to write. Don't you think the Spirit will share wisdom and understanding if you ask him for them? He wants you to know what he meant. So pray before you begin your study, and ask him to speak to you through the text.

Definition of *doctrine*: what the Bible teaches about a specific subject. For example, the doctrine of God, the doctrine of Christ, the doctrine of the church, etc.

Second, we must read the Bible in context. We can't pull out a verse and build an entire doctrine around it.

If we take verses out of context, we will create thousands of doctrines that contradict one another and really mess people up. Instead, we should look at what the original author wrote in the entire paragraph, chapter, and book in order to make sense of the individual verse.

To read the Bible in context, start by asking the right questions.

Who wrote this book?
To whom was it written?
When was it written?
What was the audience dealing with in society at the time?
Why was it written?

If you don't know the answers to those questions, many incredible and helpful resources are available to you. I've included a list of some of my favorites at the end of this book.

The reason I stress the importance of context is because without it, you'll miss so much of the meaning. Sure, you may understand the stories, but you won't understand the weight behind them. Let's look at a few examples of Scripture so you can see how important understanding the context can be.

There is a story in the Old Testament of a man named Daniel who was thrown into a lion's den (Daniel 6). If you spent any amount of time in Sunday school, you know this tale. It's all about Daniel's faith and how God delivered him from the mouths of lions who should have eaten him. But for a Jewish audience, this story was about so much more than God protecting one man. When this book was written, the Jews were in exile in Babylon. They had been ripped from their homeland and turned into slaves. Daniel worked for King Darius at the time, the king of Babylon, and the entire book of Daniel took place during this time frame. So when Daniel was protected in the lions' den, the readers understood it as both a historical fact and a broader symbol of God looking out for his people. Not only that, but the Israelites weren't allowed to pray while in exile. Daniel did anyway, and God answered his prayers. So this story encouraged readers to continue praying and remain faithful to their practices even while under foreign rule.

Or how about the Last Supper? The night before Jesus was crucified, he had dinner with his closest friends (Matthew 26). This story is beautiful, but it becomes even more impactful when you learn that the Last Supper was actually a Passover meal, deeply connected to Jewish tradition. Passover celebrates the Israelites' deliverance from slavery in Egypt and how God protected them by commanding them to mark their doorposts with the blood of a lamb so the Lord would "pass over" their homes. The Last Supper further interpreted Passover. Jesus showed them how he himself is the Lamb, whose sacrificial death would bring about a new covenant for God's people and deliver them from sin.

Today we are commanded to follow the Eucharist or Communion, as some church cultures call it. Much like the Last Supper, we eat bread and drink wine in remembrance of Jesus and the work he did on the cross.

Historical context is important, but it's not the only context to consider. We need to look at Scripture from a philosophical perspective as well. Did Jesus read the Old Testament the same way we do today in the West? Do his actions, which we read about in the Gospels, always make sense to us in our way of thinking?

Actually, no.

In the West, we view life with a Greek mindset, which is very different from the Eastern or Hebrew mindset that Jesus, the original audience, and the Bible's authors would have held. And we need to be aware of this when reading and interpreting Scripture.

We must remember that the Bible was written *for* us, but it wasn't written *to* us.

This doesn't mean we need to adopt an ancient-Eastern worldview and change the way we view life, but it does mean we need to note the differences and learn to think like Jesus would have.

So what do I mean by Greek/Western versus Hebrew/Eastern?

The Western worldview tends to focus on facts, data, and analyzing and finding proof.

The Eastern worldview tends to focus on pictures, poetry, symbolism, and story.

Greeks believed the highest level of intellect was based on linking arguments together to prove beliefs. So as the Greek mindset became dominant, thinking logically and rationally was prioritized. This mindset still dominates American perspectives.

Oftentimes we want the Bible to be scientifically accurate and logical, but the authors were trying to communicate something much deeper.

This is why we see Jesus speaking in parables so often. To us, using stories to answer questions may seem like an odd way of speaking, but to the audience, storytelling would have been a completely normal way of communicating.

Here are a few examples to help you wrap your mind around the differences:

Describing Theological Ideas	
Greek	Focuses on deep theological concepts, such as grace and propitiation
Hebrew	Focuses on images and parables to easily explain these concepts
Physical Versus Spiritual	
Greek	Separates the physical realm from the spiritual
Hebrew	Views reality holistically, with the physical and spiritual realms blended together
Holiness	
Greek	Focuses on becoming morally pure and attaining perfection
Hebrew	Focuses on the relationship with God and being set apart for his purposes
Individual Versus Communal	
Greek	Focuses on the individual's faith and need for repentance
Hebrew	Focuses on the faith of the community and how to live out the kingdom together

It's not our responsibility to entirely adopt an Eastern way of thinking about the world, but reading the Bible becomes easier when you understand the way an Eastern audience would think.[1] This comes down to *studying* and not just *reading* the Bible.

Studying Scripture should become a lifelong endeavor. We should read it and study it and talk about it and think about it as much as we can. The Bible is one of the most complex books in the world. You'll never learn everything about it, but we should develop a passion for Scripture unlike anything else.

Deuteronomy 6:7 says, "Talk about [Scripture] when you sit in your house and when you walk along the road, when you lie down and when you get up." God wants to be at the forefront of our minds, and he wants to speak to us through the Bible.

In the next chapter we'll walk through the Bible's entire storyline so when we go deeper later on, you'll be able to see where each book fits into the whole of Scripture.

One-Sentence Recap

We need to learn how to read the Bible in the original context to truly understand what is being said.

Chapter 3

The Bible Story, Simplified

One of the most important things to understand about the Bible is the overarching storyline. That way, when you read any book of the Bible, you can figure out where it fits into the bigger picture. Learning this was a game changer for me, and I know it will be for you as well.

So let's take it from the top.

In the beginning there was chaos—a time of nothingness. God's Spirit was hovering over the chaos, and God began to speak things into existence: Light. Water. Plants. Animals. Humans.

As the story goes, God placed the first two humans, Adam and Eve, in the garden of Eden. And then he gave them a task: to work the land and to make a family to expand the garden of Eden across the earth. There was only one thing they weren't allowed to do, and that was eat the fruit from the Tree of Knowledge of Good and Evil. There would be major consequences if they disobeyed.

They were left with two choices:

1. Expand the garden and maintain a perfect relationship with God.
2. Eat the fruit and choose to partner with the evil forces in the world instead.

A creature entered the scene and convinced them to eat the fruit, immediately causing a disconnect in the relationship between God and man. This is now known as the fall of humanity. Heaven and earth were essentially separated within the garden. God's presence was no longer in Adam and Eve's midst as it was before, resulting in everything going downhill.

And it got really bad. Like really, really bad. So bad that humans had no way of getting back to God's original plan. So God wiped the evil out of the world through a major flood, saving only one righteous man named Noah, his family, and a bunch of animals. The world had a fresh start.

But Noah sinned, and evil continued to spread across the world.

Along came a man named Abraham and his wife, Sarah. God chose Abraham to kick-start the redemption process of the whole world by promising to build an entire nation from Abraham's offspring. God introduced Sarah and Abraham to a new way of life: walking in partnership with God instead of trying to do everything on their own.

For the rest of the Old Testament, we learn all about Abraham and Sarah's family and their descendants. We meet Abraham's son Isaac, Isaac's son Jacob, and Jacob's twelve sons—one of whom, Joseph, was sold into slavery in Egypt. Even though that sounds like the worst thing that could've happened to Joseph, God used it for good.

The favor of God was all over Joseph's life, enabling him to rise to power within Egyptian royalty and become the pharaoh's second-in-command.

Joseph moved his brothers and father to Egypt, and over the next few centuries, the family became very large. So large, in fact, that the Egyptians were afraid they would take over the whole country. So the Egyptians enslaved Joseph's family, who by this time were a people group called the Hebrews, or Israelites.

After centuries of slavery, God raised up a deliverer for the Israelites. He was named Moses, and he performed many miracles in front of the pharaoh and commanded him to let the Israelites go.

Pharaoh wasn't easily convinced, but the Israelites were eventually allowed to leave Egypt and make their way back to the land God had promised Abraham, which was called the promised land. On this journey, they received the law from God along with plans for God's tabernacle, the physical place where he would reside with his people. The law was basically a bunch of instructions for how to live a holy life and how to approach a holy God even though the Hebrews were tainted by sin from the fall. The Ten Commandments are the most famous part of the law, but there were plenty of other instructions too.

The Israelites were organized into twelve distinct subgroups—or tribes—within the larger group. They promised to obey God, but almost immediately, they failed. As a consequence, they wandered in the wilderness for forty years until the first generation that escaped Egypt had all passed away.

After their time of wandering, Moses raised up a military leader named Joshua to take over after Moses himself died. Then Joshua successfully led the people into the promised land, organizing the groups into their designated land allotments based on the twelve different tribes.

By this time, the family had grown into millions of people. Joshua couldn't lead them all on his own, so God raised up more leaders, called judges, to help. But the people continued to disobey and chose to follow evil instead of God's plan.

Next, Israel implemented a monarchy system. King Saul was Israel's first king, followed by King David, who became Israel's greatest king. King David's son Solomon took over after David's death and built a temple for God's presence to reside in. But Solomon began to make compromises, which led to a split in the kingdom of Israel. Ten of the tribes in the North became their own kingdom, which was still called Israel. The South remained its own kingdom called Judah, consisting of two tribes, Judah and Benjamin.

None of the kings in the North followed God, and only a few in the South did. The disconnect between God and his people was growing. So God raised up prophets to warn the leaders and kings that if they didn't turn from their wicked ways, they would be led into exile.

Israel did not listen to the prophets, so exile is exactly what happened. Israel was conquered by the Babylonian army, stripped of their rights, and taken into an unknown land under the new world power.

While the Hebrews were in exile, God raised up more prophets. He communicated to and through them that one day a new leader would bring the people to their destiny and fulfill the promise God had made to Abraham all those years ago. These prophets said this new leader would come from the tribe of Judah and be a descendant of King David. They called this person the Messiah.

After Israel had spent seventy years in exile, the leader of Persia, King Cyrus, allowed them to go back to their homeland to rebuild their cities, their temple, and their relationship with God. The prophets spoke of a new covenant to come, a descendant of David who would rule forever. The Israelites took these prophecies seriously. They just didn't know when this Messiah would come.

The story then goes silent for nearly four hundred years. During this time, the Roman Empire was born and began its spread across much of the known world, including the tiny nation of Israel.

Then, all of a sudden, a prophet named John the Baptist emerged in Jerusalem. He announced that a new kingdom was at hand, and the Messiah they had all been waiting for was about to make himself known.

This man was named Jesus, from a little town called Nazareth. But Jesus didn't preach that he would take over politically or free his people from Roman oppression like everyone had expected from the Messiah. Instead he preached an upside-down kingdom, prioritizing things like loving our enemies and serving our neighbors. He healed people, cast out demons, and performed miracles to prove he was God in human form and that his kingdom was different from what was expected.

The Roman government felt threatened by Jesus because he was claiming that a new kingdom had arrived. The Jewish leaders also felt threatened because Jesus preached about a different way of doing things than what they were used to. So they persecuted Jesus from both sides. Eventually, the authorities had Jesus executed on a cross.

But in death, Jesus brought the sin of the world onto himself—and from then on, all of humanity was able to have a restored relationship with God. Jesus did for us what we couldn't do for ourselves.

Jesus rose from the dead three days later, conquering death and hell, proving that he truly was God. This event was the climax of our faith. Our beliefs as Christians are fully reliant on the belief that Jesus rose from the dead.

Jesus then commanded his friends to spread this good news all around the world. He claimed that anyone who believes in him will have their sins forgiven and become part of the kingdom of God. He left earth and returned to heaven, but he promised to return and make everything right one day.

Until then, we have the Holy Spirit inside of us. Thanks to the Spirit, we can continue being used to spread the word about the kingdom here and now, anticipating our full renewal in the future where all evil is removed and heaven and earth are united once and for all.

From the very beginning God has wanted to live in relationship with his people, with you and me. The Bible is the story of how God intended and intends to make that happen.

That's the storyline of Scripture.
That's what we're signing up for.
And praise God that he wants to include us.

One-Sentence Recap

Our relationship with God is being restored through Jesus Christ, and our role is to share the good news about his kingdom until he returns.

Part Two

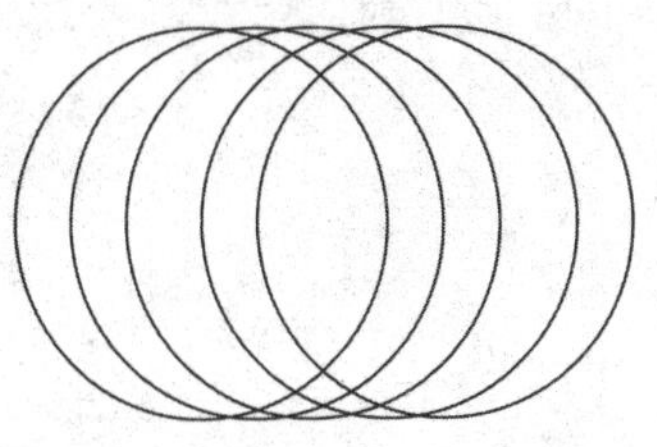

CREATION AND COVENANTS

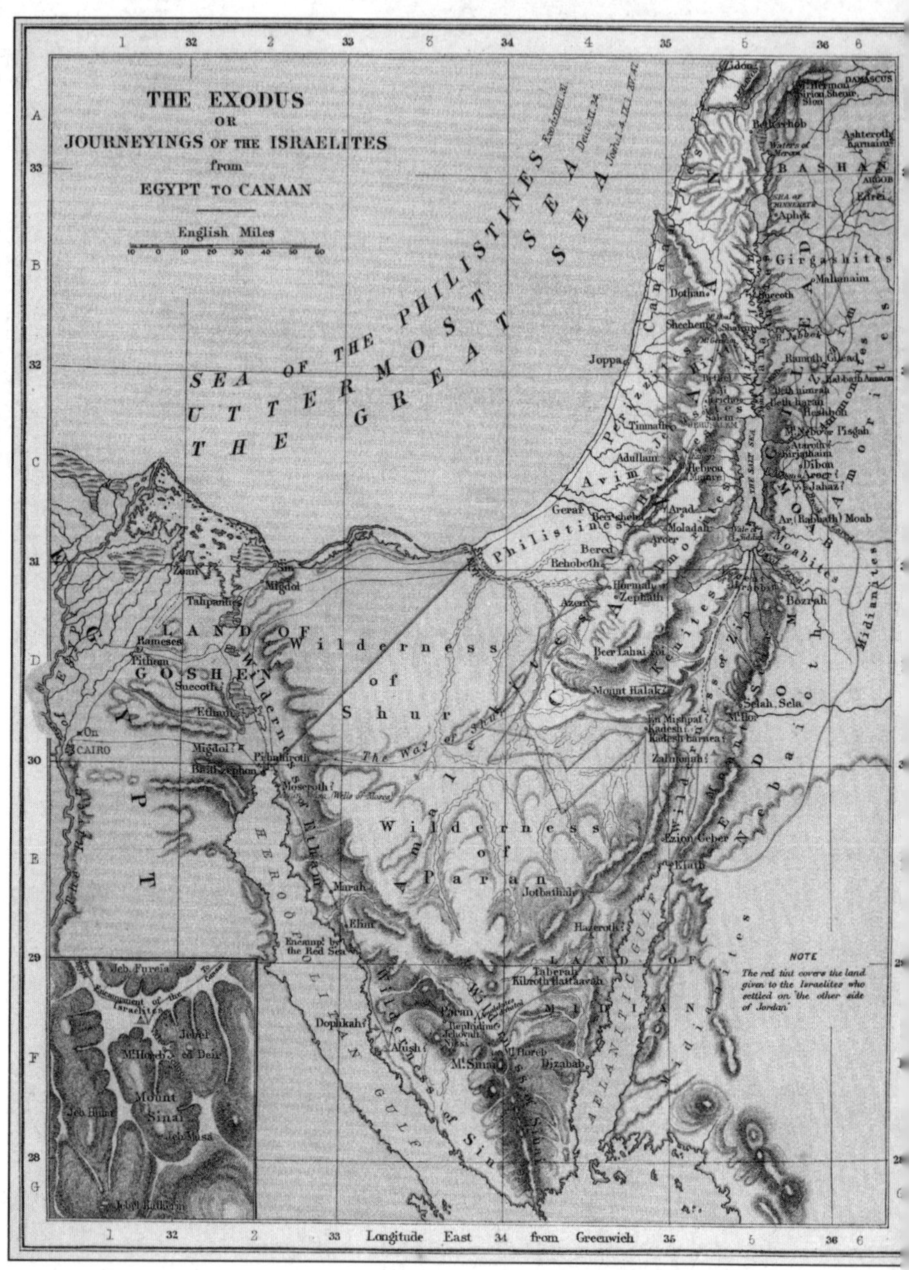

Map of the Ancient Near Eas

Chapter 4

Creation and the Fall

Genesis 1:1–3:24

This is how the Bible begins:

"In the beginning God created the heavens and the earth. Now the earth was formless and empty, darkness covered the surface of the watery depths, and the Spirit of God was hovering over the surface of the waters. Then God said, 'Let there be light,' and there was light" (Genesis 1:1–3).

If you grew up in church, these verses may go in one ear and out the other without you ever digesting what is happening here. But there is a whole lot going on, is there not? Read those verses again.

If you're like me, you now have far more questions after rereading these three sentences than you did beforehand. And this is how this very, *very* long book begins? We might be in for an epic journey here.

The author continues the story in the form of an ancient poem, by describing all that happened on the first seven days of creation.

On the first day God created the heavens and the earth. He spoke light into existence and then separated the light from the darkness. He called the light "day" and the darkness "night." And God said it was "good."

On the second day God created the sky. He separated the water on the earth from the water in the sky, creating the atmosphere.

On the third day God created dry land. He separated the water from the land, then called the land "earth" and the water "seas." He also created plants and fruit trees, covering the earth with vegetation. And God said it was good.

On the fourth day God created the sun, moon, and stars to help us keep track of time and seasons. And God said it was good.

On the fifth day God created creatures in the sea and birds in the air. And God said it was good.

On the sixth day God created all the animals that live on dry land, and then humankind. And God said they were *very* good.

On the seventh day God rested. Not because he was tired but because everything was complete. His work was finished, and now he could enjoy it.

Six days of creation, one day of rest.

Now, if you grew up in Sunday school like me, you were taught that God created the world in seven literal days. Then as you got older, you started to hear the scientific evidence that the Earth as we know it today is the result of millions of years of evolution. That might sound a little confusing and contradictory, and maybe you didn't have any Christian leaders in your life to talk to about reconciling the scientific proof for evolution with the biblical account of Genesis. You were taught to take the Bible's word for it, no matter what the evidence said. But remember: We need to learn how to read the Bible in the context and literary style in which it was written.

Could God have created the world in seven days?
Absolutely.

Did he?
I'm not sure.

But let me show you something cool about this first chapter of the Bible. Genesis 1, the creation story, was not written to be a science textbook. None of the original audience would have read it that way.

It's a poem.

Reading this poem as a science textbook misses the point of how incredible it would have been for the original audience to learn about God in this way.

So what was the author trying to teach the audience?

Well, for starters, who was the audience?

Traditionally, Genesis is thought to have been written for the Israelites at Mount Sinai after they were liberated from slavery in Egypt.

And what did the Israelites do as slaves?

They made bricks for Pharaoh. Day after day. For hundreds of years. All they knew was work; their entire identity was rooted in it.

So at the foot of Mount Sinai, God inspired Moses to write a poem teaching the Israelites that God created humans with purpose and called us "very good." God considered them even more important than the rest of creation. Not only that, but God's words taught them the importance of rest and invited them to participate in it.

This is why you'll see the idea of Sabbath repeated all throughout Scripture and why Jewish people take it so seriously. The Bible begins with a poem all about rest!

The poem continues in Genesis 2 by detailing how God created man. It says God formed him from the dust on the ground and breathed his own life, his spirit, into the man's nostrils, turning him into a living being.

God called the man Adam, which is the Hebrew word for "humanity." This shows that this story isn't just about the first man. It's about all of us.

God created Adam in his own image: to be creative like God, to reason like God, and to partner in continuing the creation process for eternity. The Bible describes God as walking and talking with Adam. They were friends.

God created a garden in Eden and placed the man in it, then invited him to cultivate the land. Inside the garden, God placed the Tree of Life, which bore fruit that allowed people to live forever. God also planted another tree called the Tree of Knowledge of Good and Evil.

When God saw Adam was lonely, he put Adam to sleep, opened his side, and fashioned a woman out of his rib. He called the woman Eve, which is the Hebrew word for "life." God also created Eve in his image, as a representation of God to the rest of the world. Men and women are equally representative of God, as they equally reflect his image.

God commanded Adam and Eve to reproduce and expand the garden all across the world, to bring God's presence and glory to the unknown. They had freedom and authority, with only one rule: God told them not to eat from the Tree of Knowledge of Good and Evil. They were able to eat from the Tree of Life and any other tree or plant inside the garden, but if they ate from the Tree of Knowledge of Good and Evil, they would die.

By placing the Tree of Knowledge of Good and Evil in the garden, God gave Adam and Eve a choice:

1. They could choose to trust in God's plan for the world and believe he knew what he was doing.
2. Or they could take things into their own hands, choosing for themselves what was good and what was evil.

Instead of forcing them to make the decision he wanted them to make, God gave them a choice. This is called "free will." He didn't create robots. He created humans to partner with. There can be no love without freedom.

Then we are introduced to a very strange being inside the garden. The Bible describes him as a serpent. But this serpent was standing upright, and he could talk.

This serpent approached Eve, questioning God's rules and whether he had *really* said what they could and couldn't eat. The serpent convinced Eve to start doubting God's instructions by saying: "You will certainly not die . . . In fact, God knows that when you eat it your eyes will be opened and you will be like God, knowing good and evil" (Genesis 3:4–5).

That's all the serpent had to say. The allure of this secret knowledge overpowered what God had said in the past. So Eve gave in to temptation, ate from the tree, and gave some fruit to Adam as well.

In this moment, everything changed for all of humanity. We call this the fall of humanity because it's the point in the story where sin entered the world, and mankind—having taken things into their own hands instead of relying on God—was left to their own devices. Evil began to take over, leading to the introduction of cancer and hurricanes and abuse and war.

Everything evil that we experience today in the world is because of sin and its consequences from generation to generation.

Immediately after the fall, Adam and Eve were kicked out of the garden and heaven was separated from earth. This was a big deal, because had they been allowed to stay in the garden, they would've had access to the Tree of Life—and eating from it would have locked them into their sinful state for all eternity. By kicking them out, God put bumpers in place to protect them from *themselves.*

But God promised to send a deliverer who would one day make everything right again.

From this point forward in the story, humanity is trapped in a downward spiral of sin—and all subsequent generations are negatively impacted by the choices of Adam and Eve.

What is sin?

Sin is anything that goes against the will of God. It comes from the Hebrew word *chata*, which means "to fail," "to miss the goal," or "to go astray."[1]

What is our goal as God's creation?

To live up to God's standards, in communion with him, fulfilling his plan for our lives.

There's a rabbinic tradition that suggests sinning is simply losing our way or forgetting who we are for a second. The belief is that by repenting, we are returning to the people we were originally created to be: our real selves. Repenting is about turning 180 degrees from our sin and walking in the opposite direction, away from the serpent and toward God.

The consequences of the fall are still impacting us all these years later. As

Christians, we believe God sent his Son, Jesus, to redeem our relationship with him. Jesus was the promised deliverer. As Christians, we have a hope for the future in which he will return, completely restoring and redeeming everything in the new heaven and new earth, destroying evil and sin for good.

We'll get to that part of the story soon. But for now, we're still on Adam, Eve, and the fall of humanity. Next you'll see how far down they spiraled as a family.

One-Sentence Recap

God created the world so he could live in community with humanity, but Adam and Eve chose to go against God's will, which led to sin entering the world.

How to Find Jesus in This Story

Jesus is the promised deliverer who has redeemed humanity by placing them back into right relationship with God.

How to Apply This Lesson to Your Life

We must repent from our sins in order to return to the people we were originally created to be.

Chapter 5

Cain and Abel

Genesis 4:1–16

Adam and Eve were banished from the garden of Eden so they wouldn't get locked into a sinful state for eternity and mess things up even further for humanity. God allowed present pain in order to foster true redemption in the future.

In Genesis 4 we are introduced to Adam and Eve's first son, Cain. The Bible teaches us that Cain grew up working the soil, meaning that he was a farmer and gardener. Then Adam and Eve had a second son named Abel, who chose to be a shepherd.

Even though the family was now outside the garden of Eden, they still had a relationship with God and knew how invested he was in the work they did. Whether relying on God for rain and sunshine for their crops (like Cain did) or for protection and health for their flocks (like Abel did), humanity's first family understood God's intimate involvement with their work.

The first act of worship we learn about in Scripture is an offering given to God by both Cain and Abel. Cain put together some fruit from the ground and presented it to the Lord. It wasn't the first of his crop, and it sure wasn't his best. It was an ordinary offering.

Abel, however, presented God with an offering of the first of his flock. He demonstrated how much he respected God by giving him the best of what he had.

Two offerings.
One was the first and the best.
One was ordinary.
Both were accepted by God.

But God liked Abel's offering better because it was more valuable. Abel's heart was fully in it. God always favors the best of the best.

Cain didn't like that his younger brother was getting more attention from God, so he became angry and jealous. But God wasn't mad at Cain for his offering. In fact, God came to him and said, "Why are you angry? Why is your face downcast? If you do what is right, will you not be accepted? But if you do not do what is right, sin is crouching at your door; it desires to have you, but you must rule over it" (Genesis 4:6–7 NIV).

It's as if God was saying, "This time, I liked your brother's offering more than yours. You will have another chance to make it right, so don't stress about it."

God was offering Cain a choice, just as he had with Adam and Eve. He could choose one way and be blessed, or he could choose another and give in to the desires of his heart. Cain was handed the opportunity to rewrite his negative feelings of jealousy and turn them into a positive force.

God was saying, "Will you choose to do good or not?" It was a test. God still had hope for Cain. He didn't reject him.

But Cain didn't listen to God. He still felt like he wasn't good enough and allowed his insecurities to get the best of him. The next time Cain and Abel were out in the field together, Cain let his anger and jealousy win. When he killed Abel, it was the first murder.

If you play stupid games, you win stupid prizes. God cursed Cain so that all the work he put into growing crops would no longer provide for him. He was banished to the East to become a wanderer in the land, removed even farther from Eden and God's presence. You'll notice how separation from God becomes the greatest downfall for the people in Scripture. And the East is often the place of refuge.

We also see that God was still merciful. He marked Cain with a sign of his protection over him, as a warning to anyone who might try to avenge Abel's death by attacking Cain. God punished Cain, but he did not abandon him.

Cain's choice is echoed throughout Scripture and the rest of history. Like Cain, you can choose to do what is right, or you can choose to do evil and give in to the ways of the Enemy. In the New Testament, John says, "This is how we know who the children of God are and who the children of the devil are: Anyone who does not do what is right is not God's child, nor is anyone who does not love their brother or sister. For this is the message you heard from the beginning: We should love one another. Do not be like Cain, who belonged to the Evil One and murdered his brother. And why did he murder him? Because his own actions were evil and his brother's were righteous" (1 John 3:10–12).

We are still presented with this choice today.

Can I show you something really interesting here? After God cursed Cain, the author included a long genealogy. For us modern Christians, genealogies can feel like a waste of space. But for an ancient Jewish audience, the genealogy was thrilling. It showed so much more of the story. In this case, we learn about how civilization was developed through the line of Adam.

Adam and Eve then had another son named Seth. Eve said, "God has given me another offspring in place of Abel, since Cain killed him" (Genesis 4:25). God gave her a replacement for the good seed.

Cain was the seed of the snake, polluted by the Evil One.
Seth was the new seed under Eve, the hope of the future.

In Judaism, a name wasn't (and isn't) just a label. Some names said good things about the person. Some were a little disturbing. A name back then told a story about one's character or destiny, and as we read about people in the Bible today, their names can add an extra layer to our understanding.

Seth's name was no different. The root of Seth is "foundation," meaning Seth was going to be a fresh start for Eve's seed. God would build a new foundation through Seth's line. It's only fitting, then, that we find out Seth's son is named Enosh. Enosh meant "human," just like Adam meant "human." But the name Enosh put more of an emphasis on the frailty of humanity.[1] Not only that, but at this moment in Scripture, we learn how the people began "to call upon the name of the LORD" (Genesis 4:26 NASB). In other words, they began to pray.

A new foundation was put into place through Seth, and a new humanity was being built through Enosh: a family of worshippers fully dedicated to and dependent on God.

This story presents us with a choice. We can choose to do things either God's way or our own way.

Which one will you choose?

One-Sentence Recap

The first recorded murder is of Cain killing Abel in an act of jealousy toward his brother.

How to Find Jesus in This Story

Just as Abel brought his best sacrifice to God, Jesus is the perfect sacrifice for us. By adopting his sacrifice as our own, we can be made righteous in God's eyes.

How to Apply This Lesson to Your Life

If you choose God's way instead of the ways of the world, he will bless you and place favor on your life.

Chapter 6

Noah and the Flood

Genesis 6:11–9:19

The Bible is funny because when we flip one page, hundreds of years can fly by. In this case, ten generations passed between the time of Adam and a time of evil so extreme that God regretted making humans in the first place. In response to the evil, God decided to wipe humanity out completely and restart the world.

The story introduces us to a man named Noah. Noah was a righteous man, and he had a close, personal relationship with God. Humanity needed a fresh start, and God wanted Noah to be the blueprint.

So God commanded Noah to build a massive boat to house his wife, his three sons, their wives, and two of each animal.

Noah obeyed without questioning God. Don't you think if you were in his shoes, you'd have a lot of questions? Like,

God, you're going to do what?

And it's going to wipe out who?

And you're only going to save us?

Isn't that a little aggressive?

But God commanded and Noah obeyed. He began building.

For 120 years Noah built an ark to God's exact specifications. You would expect people to question Noah about why he was building such a large ark. And then you might wonder what his response might be. Did Noah tell them to repent because God was going to wipe out the world? Or did Noah remain silent since the damage had already been done? We don't know.

Once Noah was finished building the ark, he loaded it up with his family and two of each animal, one male and one female.

And it began to rain. One drop, two drops, and then a downpour for what the Bible describes as forty days and forty nights. The number forty is symbolic throughout the Bible, often connected with purification and new life. The flood eventually lifted the ark up off the ground.

As the waters rose, everything died.

Everything was gone except one little family and the foundation of a new creation.

In the Western world, we look at stories like this and want to know the science behind them. We approach a natural occurrence and want to know *how* God did it. But that's not the way the original audience would have understood this story. We need to read it for what it is: an ancient document communicating to an ancient world.

The simple truth is that ancient people wrote stories about floods. This story isn't unique to Judaism. There was a famous Mesopotamian flood story, a Sumerian one, and African and Egyptian and Caledonian and Babylonian ones. Many cultures in the Ancient Near East had a story that involved a flood. They also had stories about the world being in shambles and the gods wiping out humanity in order to start anew.

The fact that other flood stories exist can sometimes feel threatening to Christians. They worry that comparing Noah's flood to other, mythological accounts cheapens the story we have in Genesis. I think the comparison actually gives weight to our story. Let me explain.

After the water surged on the earth for 150 days, God remembered Noah, his family, and the animals. He caused a wind to pass over the water, and the water began to subside. Does this sound familiar? The "wind" here is the same word for "spirit" that we learned about in Genesis 1, when the spirit hovered over the waters before God began to speak things into existence. This is meant to be a direct parallel.

In Genesis, the waters were divided, the land came forth, the animals were created, and humans followed.

In the story of Noah, the water subsides, the land emerges, the raven and the dove go out, and the animals and people inhabit the land.

This was a return to order. God was doing a new thing.

And what was the first thing Noah did when he stepped off the boat? He built an altar to God, then praised him for their deliverance and the ability to start over in relationship with him. Noah lived a life of reverence and worship. We should be inspired to do the same.

Now, this is where the story really stands above the other ancient texts. You see, the other stories are all about destruction and violence. Everyone dies, and the gods are happy about it.

Our God is different.

Our God made a covenant with Noah, promising to never wipe out the earth again. He wanted a relationship with Noah, just like he wanted a relationship with Adam and Eve. This was a completely new way of thinking about the divine. The original audience wouldn't have ever heard anything like this before. The false gods most people worshipped wanted nothing to do with them. The God of the Bible actually *cared* about his people. He *loved* them.

So God blessed Noah and his children, commanding them to "be fruitful and multiply and fill the earth" (Genesis 9:1). Sound familiar?

Noah is the new Adam here.
Everything is back in its place.
Order has been established again.
And the future is dripping with hope.

One-Sentence Recap

God saved Noah, his family, and the animals from a flood that was intended to wipe out the wickedness of humanity and renew creation.

How to Find Jesus in This Story

Jesus is the ultimate salvation, offering us deliverance from the judgment of the world through his sacrifice.

How to Apply This Lesson to Your Life

Noah found favor because he was obedient, blameless, and had an intimate relationship with God. We should focus on those three things as well.

Chapter 7

The Tower of Babel

Genesis 11:1–9

Even though Noah and his family served as humanity's reboot, sin was still deeply ingrained in our nature thanks to the fall. There was no way to get away from it. Noah sinned right away after creating his covenant with God, and sin took hold of their family and all people to come.

Noah's three sons were named Shem, Ham, and Japheth, and since Noah was the new Adam, every person through the rest of Scripture can be traced back to these ancestors. Noah's son Ham had a son named Nimrod, which means "rebel" in Hebrew.

And Nimrod lived up to his name.

Instead of obeying God's command to spread out into the world, Nimrod wanted the people to come together and become a great nation by themselves—all without the help of God. So the tribe of Nimrod settled in an area called Shinar, which is about fifty-five miles south of Baghdad today. There, they began to build a city called Babylon. (This city will be brought up a lot as we make our way through Scripture.)

The people of Babylon were smart. They were made in God's image, just like you and I. The Babylonians were industrious and built one of the most advanced cities in the ancient world. It may sound funny to us today, but one of their greatest technological advancements was the creation of the brick.

God didn't have a problem with them inventing bricks, but what they chose to do with the bricks would either benefit them or lead them to destruction—choosing good or choosing bad.

Under Nimrod's leadership, they chose destruction.

Instead of making bricks in abundance to help struggling people, the Babylonians chose to build a great city, along with a massive tower in the middle of it with the goal of reaching the heavens.

They wanted to make a name for themselves.

They wanted to be *great*.

Josephus, a great historian during the time of Jesus, wrote, "He [Nimrod] also said he would be revenged on God, if he should have a mind to drown the world again; for that he would build a tower too high for the waters to be able to reach! and that he would avenge himself on God for destroying their forefathers!"[1]

Everything Nimrod did was an act of rebellion toward God.

The Babylonians wanted to show how great they were as a people and how their creation could join heaven and earth together. In the eyes of their neighbors, the Babylonians had a bridge between heaven and earth that could be crossed whenever they pleased. The Babylonians thought they were essentially on the same level as the gods themselves.

But their pride and arrogance would be their downfall.

Who were they to believe they could compete on God's playing field?

After Adam and Eve lost access to the garden of Eden—the *true* bridge between heaven and earth—this group of people were now trying to restore the overlap for themselves.

God said, "If as one people speaking the same language they have begun to do this, then nothing they plan to do will be impossible for them" (Genesis 11:6 NIV).

God didn't have a problem with them building a city or a tower. What he took issue with was the arrogance that came along with it. The Babylonians thought they could be in charge of the connection between heaven and earth. But in reality, God has ultimate control.

So God scattered the people himself, confusing their language and putting a halt to their arrogance. He made it so the Babylonians started speaking different languages, which removed their ability to communicate and introduced different languages into the world.

God stepped in to help them, not to harm them. There's nothing wrong with speaking a different language. Instead of destroying all of humanity as he did with the flood, God chose to scatter them. The people who could still communicate with one another broke off into their own communities and began to spread across the world.

Afterward, the city became known as Babel. Now, there is wordplay going on here, because in Hebrew the root of the word *babel* means "to jumble or confuse." But the inhabitants of Babylon interpreted the word to mean "the gate of the gods." Isn't that interesting? How one culture can view an area as a confusing mess, while another culture sees it as the bridge between heaven and earth, between gods and man?[2]

The whole Bible—and our whole history, for that matter—is all about the kingdom of God versus the kingdom of evil: Jerusalem versus

Babylon, Eden versus the world, light versus darkness, good versus bad, peace versus chaos, love versus hate, humility versus pride.

And as humans, we get to choose who deserves our allegiance. We can choose God's way, which results in eternal life, or we can choose the way of the world, which leads to death. With pure hearts, our lives can be bridges between heaven and earth, and everywhere we go, we can bring the kingdom of God with us.

In the next chapter we are going to learn about covenants and how God chose specific individuals to partner with as he brought his kingdom to earth.

One-Sentence Recap

The story of Babel demonstrates how a group of people tried to build a city and tower that reached the heavens in rebellion to God's plan, resulting in the confusion of their language and their scattering across the earth.

How to Find Jesus in This Story

Jesus is the one who reverses the confusion of languages and division among humans by uniting people through the gospel message.

How to Apply This Lesson to Your Life

This story shows us what happens when we let pride control our lives. Instead we should seek humility and dependence on God, in hopes of working together for his ultimate purpose.

Chapter 8

Introduction to Covenants

In order to bring your knowledge of the Bible to another level, let's take a quick break from the storyline and discuss covenants.

A covenant is simply an agreement made between two people (or tribes or nations) to work together for a specific purpose. Those who enter a covenant promise to do their part for the collective good. It's basically a deal, but with a lot more weight behind it.

Now, not all covenants are created equal.

Some covenants are conditional, meaning that each party must do exactly what they said they would do. If one side doesn't hold up their end of the deal, then the covenant is broken.

On the other hand, some covenants are unconditional, meaning the promise will stick no matter what the other party does. In the Bible, we see a lot of unconditional covenants.

I'll first explain the covenant process, and then I'll show you examples from the Bible. This is where it gets really interesting.

In the ancient world, it was common to "cut" a covenant. This isn't just Bible talk; it was a cultural practice. And since the Bible is written to a specific culture, it was normal life for them. Creating a covenant with someone involved an entire ritual, and while the details of this ritual may strike us as odd, the original readers would have understood the imagery.

A covenant-cutting session began with the sacrifice of an animal. First, the two people entering the covenant would choose a spotless animal and work together as a team to cut the animal in half lengthwise (like a hot dog, not a hamburger). This alone would've been a bloody, smelly, sweaty, dirty process. They would then lay each half of the animal side by side with enough room to walk between the halves.

Second, representatives of each party (family, friends, etc.) would stand behind each side of the animal to witness the covenant taking place. The two parties would then walk between the halves of the animal to signify that they were passing through death to enter a lifelong commitment with the other person.

Third, blood from the animal would be sprinkled on both parties.

Fourth, they would both speak the terms of the covenant aloud, suggesting that they would become like the animal if they didn't live up to their end of the deal. This was serious business. Life-or-death type stuff.

Lastly, they would share a celebratory meal to symbolize the new family they had created through this contract.

As wild and gory as that may seem to us today, it was typical for the people in the Bible. So we see God doing the exact same thing in Scripture because his people would have understood the significance of the event.

A few chapters ago we learned about Adam and Eve and how they chose to do things on their own, apart from God's original plan. Evil spread throughout the land and things got really bad for a bit because of the broken relationship God had with humans. So now, instead of focusing on a relationship with humanity as a whole, God chose to partner with individuals who would positively influence the rest of humanity. He made covenants with them and held up his end of the bargains, even if the individuals failed to hold up their ends.

God makes five major covenants throughout Scripture.

Noahic covenant
Abrahamic covenant
Mosaic covenant
Davidic covenant
New covenant

We haven't discussed most of these people yet, but being aware of them now will help you make more sense of things when we get to them later.

Noahic Covenant (Genesis 9:8–17)

The first of the five major covenants was the Noahic covenant: God's covenant with Noah.

Right after the flood, God promised Noah that he would never destroy humanity again by flood. This was an unconditional covenant, a promise God would keep no matter how crazy things got in the world. God even placed a rainbow in the sky, which Noah and his descendants saw as a symbol of this covenant.

God invited Noah and his family to partner with him on filling the world with his goodness, in proper relationship, the way God intended. Noah ended up failing shortly after, but God has continued to hold up his end of the deal.

Abrahamic Covenant (Genesis 15:1–21; 17:1–14)

God blessed Abraham by promising to give him more descendants than he could ever imagine, along with land for them to live in. And through Abraham, God planned to bless the rest of the world.

This covenant was unconditional, but God did command Abraham to raise his family in the way of God and always do what was right. The sign of the Noahic covenant was a rainbow, and Abraham's covenant had a sign too—although it was a little, let's say, different. The sign of this covenant was circumcision. Can you imagine what was running through Abraham's mind when God let him in on this little detail? Were the blessings worth it? He might've wondered, *Why can't I have a rainbow in the clouds like Noah?* But no, every descendant of Abraham was to be circumcised.

Mosaic Covenant (Exodus 24:1–8)

Abraham's family grew, just as God promised. It grew so big that the Egyptian people were afraid they would take over Egypt, so they enslaved the Israelites for four hundred years. God raised up Moses to liberate them from oppression.

Once they were free, God met with Moses on Mount Sinai and gave him the Ten Commandments along with the rest of the law. God commanded the people to follow these rules and promised to bless them if they were faithful. This was a conditional covenant—one that required both parties to uphold their ends of the deal.

Davidic Covenant (2 Samuel 7:12–16)

When the nation of Israel moved to a monarchy style of government, David became their second and greatest king. Life under King David was somewhat of a golden age for the Israelites.

God cut an unconditional covenant with David that would one day benefit all of humankind. He promised that a new king would arise from David's descendants—one whose kingdom would last forever.

New Covenant (Jeremiah 31:31–34)

While the nation of Israel was in exile, God spoke through a group of prophets. He promised that a new, eternal covenant would one day redeem their relationship with God and bless not just the Israelites but the whole entire world. These prophets spoke of a new king who would come from the line of David and lead them to freedom, not just physically but spiritually.

The New Testament introduces the person who would lead the way with this new covenant. Jesus was fully human and fully God, and he came to earth to renew humanity's broken relationship with God and fulfill both sides of the covenant. Now whoever believes in Jesus and accepts his sacrifice as their own can become part of God's covenantal family.

Understanding all of this is crucial for understanding the storyline of the Bible. This extra layer of insight will bring so much more clarity to our Western minds as we continue on with the story.

One-Sentence Recap

A biblical covenant is a deal made between God and humanity with the goal of working together to renew the world.

How to Find Jesus in This Story

Jesus presents us with a new covenant that allows humanity to be in right relationship with God again.

How to Apply This Lesson to Your Life

By accepting Jesus, you are now in a covenantal relationship with God to spread his kingdom and provide hope for humanity. That's a major deal! When you understand the weight of covenants, you should feel inspired to live with a new sense of godly pride.

Chapter 9

Abraham, Isaac, and Jacob

Genesis 12–50

Can you imagine leaving everything behind just because God told you to?

Like, *everything* everything. Your family, your job, the city you grew up in, your comfort zone—everything.

It sounds like such a brave thing to do, and a lot of you are probably thinking, *Yeah, if God himself was calling me to do that, I would* . . . I'd like to think I would too. But I'm sure leaving everything behind is a lot easier said than done.

Abram was a seventy-five-year-old man from a city called Ur in southern Mesopotamia. Like most people in that time, he lived with his whole family. For them, family was everything. People didn't move away to chase their dreams or see a new part of the world. A father did a specific trade for work, and then his sons followed in his footsteps to carry on the legacy.

Abram eventually moved to Haran, which meant he was surrounded by polytheism. Basically everyone Abram knew would have believed in a lot of different gods. They didn't have other religious options; it was just the way things were. In a polytheist society, people served the gods with all they had, although the gods were nearly impossible to please.

But Abram was different. He served the one true God and him alone, opposing the idolatry of the surrounding culture. By believing in the God of heaven, Abram was completely countercultural and righteous in the eyes of God.

So when the Bible drops in on this conversation between Abram and God, we should acknowledge that God was asking Abram to do something that simply wasn't done: leave his family for an unknown adventure. God told Abram that if he obeyed, he would receive three things:

1. A land of his own
2. A blessing on his whole family
3. A great nation who would bless every other nation as his legacy

We have the supreme God reaching out directly to one man and promising blessings if he was obedient to the calling God placed on his life. God planned to use this one man to build a community of righteous people and change the world for good—if Abram was willing.

So Abram left town with his wife, Sarai, his nephew Lot, and all their possessions to go to an unknown land: Canaan.

Abram traveled through Shechem and Bethel and the Negev, and as the days, weeks, and months dragged on, he started questioning God's call on his life. Sometimes he made mistakes, took matters into his own hands, or lied to get out of trouble. At one point, things got so tense that Lot split off and settled in an area called Sodom, away from Abram's immediate family.

In Bethel, God reinforced his promise to Abram. God told Abram to bring together a heifer, a goat, a ram, a dove, and a young pigeon. Culturally, Abram would have known exactly what to do here. God was making a covenant with him.

So Abram cut the animals in half, just as anybody at the time would've done in preparation for the covenant—but instead of Abram walking through the middle and committing to his part, God put Abram to sleep and walked through in the form of a smoking firepot and a blazing torch. This symbolized the unconditional nature of the covenant. It wasn't dependent on anything Abram said or did. It was dependent on God's faithfulness.

By this point, Abram and Sarai were getting old and still didn't have any children of their own—let alone enough offspring to make God's promised "great nation." So they took the situation into their own hands. Sarai had Abram sleep with her servant, Hagar, and Hagar got pregnant with a son, Ishmael. Remember Ishmael, because he becomes the father of his own nation, and they become a very important group in both the Bible and the world.

Around this time, God changed Abram's name to Abraham and Sarai's name to Sarah. Abraham means "father of a multitude." God was reminding Abraham to keep trusting him—as if he were saying, "Yes, you will be the father of a great nation one day, and you will be given the land I promised you."

A year later, Sarah gave birth to Abraham's son, just as God promised. They named him Isaac.

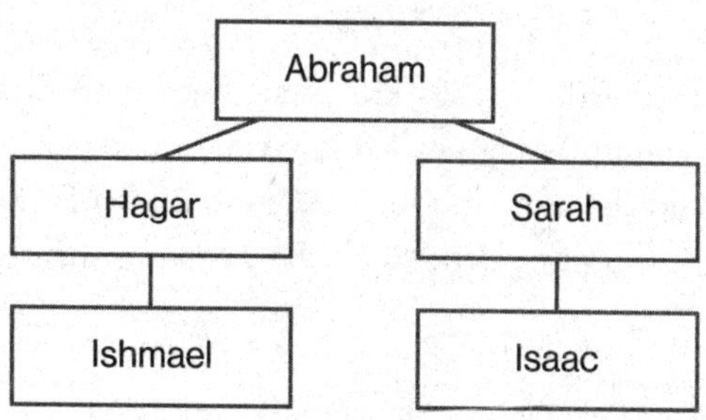

Isaac was Abraham and Sarah's pride and joy. He was the fruition of God's promise, when Abraham was nearly a hundred years old. Abraham's legacy would be built through this boy. All of God's promises were being fulfilled.

But Abraham was about to be put to the most devastating test imaginable. As Isaac grew from a little boy to a young man, God called Abraham and asked him to take Isaac up to Mount Moriah and sacrifice him.

God told Abraham to kill his promised child.

This sounds shocking, but in ancient times, it wasn't unheard of. Most of the cultures in the area sacrificed children to their false gods in hopes of being blessed with a multitude of others, so such sacrifices were considered normal.

But Abraham's God was different. He just didn't know that yet.

So Abraham began to take Isaac up to the place God told him to go with an armful of wood and a knife. When they arrived at the location God had commanded, Abraham told Isaac to get on the altar himself. Can you imagine the look on Isaac's face at this point? Did he also have the faith of Abraham?

We don't know how the conversation went down, but we do know that Abraham raised his knife with the intent to kill his son, just as God had requested. Then, all of a sudden, God made himself known and stopped Abraham.

This God was different from the other gods.

He never wanted Abraham to kill Isaac, but he needed to know if Abraham was committed or not—if he could be obedient to the call no matter how wild the request. God needed to know if Abraham cared more about the promise or the One who gave him the promise in the first place.

And Abraham passed the test.

His faith was greater.

Abraham was prepared to obey God, but at the last minute, God spared Isaac's life.

He provided Abraham with a ram for the sacrifice instead.

Abraham went against his personal desires and trusted God's plan over his own. Because of his obedience, Isaac grew up, got married to a woman named Rebekah, and eventually had his own sons: Jacob and Esau.

A prophecy was spoken over Rebekah while she was pregnant. God told her: "Two nations are in your womb; two peoples will come from you and be separated. One people will be stronger than the other, and the older will serve the younger" (Genesis 25:23). Rebekah held this close to her heart and tried to imagine what the future would hold.

As Jacob and Esau got older, they took on roles that suited their talents. Esau was a hunter and spent most of his time out in the fields, providing for his family. Jacob was more of a homebody.

Esau was the firstborn, which meant he was the inheritor of Isaac's blessing and all he had built.

He was a strong, outdoorsy type. He was his father's favorite. Meanwhile, Jacob developed a love of cooking and grew closer to his mother. Based on the prophecy she'd heard, Rebekah knew Jacob would one day be in charge.

Jacob wasn't as strong as his older brother, but he was sly and crafty. As the firstborn, Esau had a special responsibility to take over the family business one day—a responsibility called a birthright. But Jacob tricked him out of his birthright by taking advantage of Esau's hasty nature;

Jacob simply traded a pot of his famous stew for his elder brother's birthright.

By this point, Isaac was very old, and it was time to give his blessing to his firstborn son, Esau. A "blessing" to the firstborn was a major deal. Isaac would have been thinking through this blessing for a very long time because, in his mind, his words would become the world his children would live in.

But Rebekah was rooting for Jacob, so she put together a plan to help her favorite son receive the blessing instead. She tied goatskin on Jacob's arms and neck to imitate Esau's hairy body. She also helped Jacob make Isaac's favorite food. Isaac was blind and slightly senile, so Rebekah knew that if they did everything right, Isaac wouldn't be able to tell the difference between his two sons.

Jacob did as his mother told him, and the trick worked. Isaac was deceived, and Jacob received his blessing. Isaac said: "From the dew of heaven and the richness of the earth, may God always give you abundant harvests of grain and bountiful new wine. May many nations become your servants, and may they bow down to you. May you be the master over your brothers, and may your mother's sons bow down to you. All who curse you will be cursed, and all who bless you will be blessed" (Genesis 27:28–29 NLT).

And that was it. Jacob officially received the blessing of the firstborn over his brother, Esau. He was truly living up to his name at this point: Jacob means "the deceiver."

Esau wasn't too happy about all this. In fact, he vowed to take revenge on Jacob by killing him, so Jacob ran to his mother's hometown and moved in with his uncle for a few years. While there, he married his uncle's two daughters: Leah and Rachel. The Bible tells us that Jacob really loved Rachel and wasn't nearly as into Leah. However, Leah ended up being the mother of most of Jacob's children.

This is when Abraham's family really began to grow.

This is what their family tree looked like:

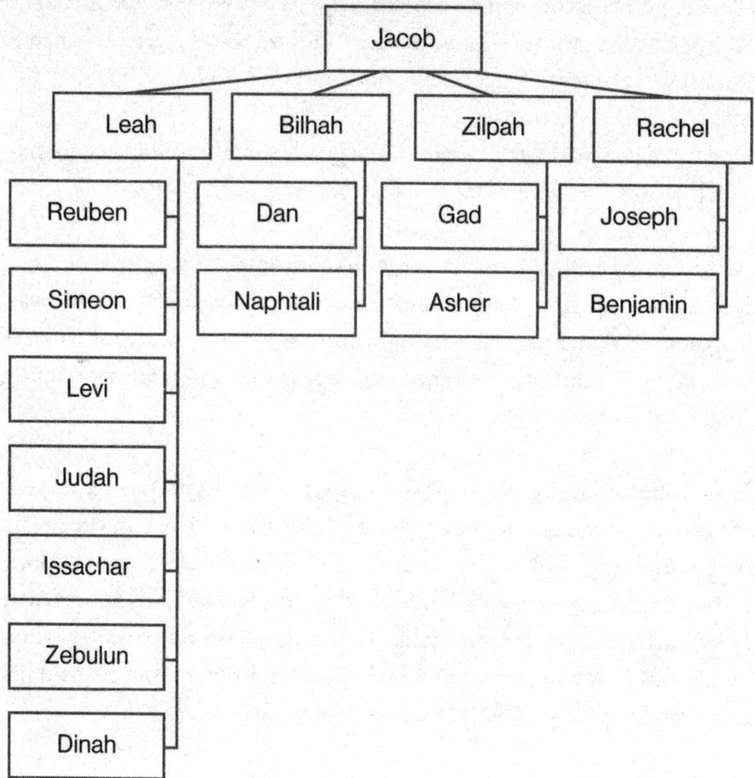

Leah gave birth to Reuben, Simeon, Levi, and Judah.

Rachel, upset that she hadn't been able to get pregnant, told Jacob to sleep with her servant, Bilhah. Sound familiar? The same thing happened between Abraham and Sarah and her servant Hagar.

Bilhah gave birth to Dan and Naphtali.

Then Leah asked Jacob to conceive with her servant, Zilpah, and she gave birth to Gad and Asher.

Leah ended up having three more children herself: Issachar, Zebulun, and finally a girl named Dinah.

By this point, Jacob had eleven children (ten boys and one girl), and Rachel was the mother of none of them. He and Rachel were devastated. Rachel was the love of Jacob's life, not Leah or Bilhah or Zilpah.

God finally opened Rachel's womb and gave them one son named Joseph. You'll want to remember Joseph. Joseph was special.

After many years, Jacob decided to take his large family, his servants, and all their livestock back home where he'd grown up. But on the way, he got word that Esau was coming with four hundred warriors to meet him. Jacob naturally figured that Esau was still furious and was coming to settle the score.

Jacob split his family into two groups, so that if one group got attacked, the other could make a break for it. Then he waited alone in the desert for Esau's army. As Jacob spent the night in fear of what was to come, he had an encounter with God. A man (or an angel of God) approached Jacob and fought with him for the entire night, blow for blow, wrestling in the desert. We know Jacob wasn't much of a fighter, but he held his own for a long time. Finally, the man said to Jacob:

> "Let me go, for it is daybreak."
> But Jacob said, "I will not let you go unless you bless me."
> "What is your name?" the man asked.
> "Jacob," he replied.
> "Your name will no longer be Jacob," he said. "It will be Israel because you have struggled with God and with men and have prevailed."
> (Genesis 32:26–28)

Jacob, the deceiver, was having his identity rewritten. He would no longer be called the deceiver; God renamed him "someone who wrestles with God." This would not only become *his* identity but also the identity of the entire nation he would give birth to.

After Jacob got up from wrestling with God, he saw Esau on the horizon, coming his way with an army of men who could've easily destroyed all he had built. Jacob was prepared for the worst, but the story takes a turn. God had a different plan. Esau and Jacob reunited and, in one of the most touching scenes in the whole Bible, Esau forgave Jacob for his betrayal all those years ago. No anger or animosity lasted between them, just brotherly love after being apart for so long. All was well.

On Jacob's way home, Rachel went into labor with Jacob's twelfth son, but it didn't go well. As she struggled to survive, she asked Jacob to name her son Ben-oni, meaning "son of my suffering." But instead, Jacob called him Benjamin, meaning "son of my right hand." Sadly, Rachel died during this childbirth, and Benjamin became Jacob's other prized child, along with Joseph.

We'll learn more about Joseph, Benjamin, and Jacob's other sons in the next chapter.

One-Sentence Recap

Abraham's faithfulness to his covenant with God paved the way for God's plan of salvation, and Jacob's life of deceit and conflict transformed into the fulfillment of God's promises; then his identity was changed as God renamed him Israel.

How to Find Jesus in This Story

Not only is Jesus a descendant of Abraham, but through Jesus we see the fulfillment of God's promise to Abraham in Jesus' death and resurrection.

How to Apply This Lesson to Your Life

God wants to use people who are willing to leave everything behind and fight for what they believe in, just like he did with Abraham and his family.

Chapter 10

Joseph

Genesis 37–50

The Bible says Jacob loved his son Joseph more than the other eleven because he was the firstborn of Rachel, his one true love. And with his love for Joseph came favor and blessings that the other boys didn't receive.

Not only that, but it was clear that Joseph had a special connection with God too. He was exceptionally bright, and God spoke to him through dreams, even giving him the ability to interpret dreams for others. Joseph would often share his dreams with his brothers, which made them hate him even more since the dreams were always positive for Joseph and discouraging for the others.

One day Jacob asked Joseph to go check on his brothers while they were working. As he was still way off in the distance, his brothers, fed up with his entitled treatment, decided to jump him and throw him down into a pit. They tore up the fancy multicolored coat that his dad had given him, and later, when a group of Ishmaelites (descendants of Abraham and Hagar's son, Ishmael) happened by on their way to Egypt, they sold Joseph to them as a slave. This is how Joseph went from being the prized son of a well-respected patriarch to a foreign slave in a country where no one knew his name.

In Egypt, the Ishmaelites sold Joseph to a man named Potiphar, one of Pharaoh's officials who ruled as captain of the guard. The Lord placed his grace on the life of Joseph, making it obvious to Potiphar that this boy was special. Potiphar placed Joseph in charge of his entire household, knowing that if God was with Joseph, the household was in good hands. Joseph was still a servant, but things were looking up.

As Joseph grew older, he turned out to be not only bright but handsome. He was so handsome that Potiphar's wife tried to seduce him, and when Joseph turned her down, she accused him of attacking her. So Potiphar had Joseph thrown in jail.

But the Lord remained with Joseph, even inside the prison. Joseph was a trustworthy and likable guy, and he was loved by both the prison guards and his fellow prisoners. Joseph even helped interpret some of the other prisoners' dreams. And after one of those prisoners was set free by the pharaoh, he remembered Joseph's spiritual gift of dream interpretation.

Years later, Pharaoh had very strange dreams of his own. He sent for his wisemen and magicians to help him interpret what he'd experienced, but nobody could figure out what the dreams meant. But then one of Joseph's old prison buddies heard the pharaoh needed someone who could interpret dreams, and he had just the guy. Pharaoh called for Joseph to be brought to him. With God's help, Joseph immediately interpreted Pharaoh's dreams as warnings of a coming famine that would devastate all of Egypt if actions weren't taken to prepare for hardship.

Pharaoh not only believed Joseph, but he also recognized how special Joseph was. He tasked Joseph with preparing the nation for a mass famine by storing enough grain and crops to last through the coming lean years. This promotion meant Joseph was now second-in-command in all the land.

Under Joseph's command, the granaries and stock houses overflowed with food and supplies for seven years, just as God had said.

Soon everything changed in the land. The famine began to spread, impacting the surrounding nations. People were dying, animals were dying, and nobody had food except for Egypt. So everyone in the neighboring regions had to travel to Egypt to buy food.

Including Joseph's family.

One day, nearly twenty-two years after Joseph was sold into slavery, his brothers arrived in Egypt to buy grain. And just as Joseph's uncle, Esau, forgave his brother, Jacob, years before, Joseph forgave his brothers for their own actions. In fact, he had his whole family brought near Egypt so they could be more easily provided for until the years of famine ended.

Joseph's family thrived in the land, growing bigger and bigger and turning into a powerful nation of Israelites. But the good times were not to last, as we'll see in the next chapter.

One-Sentence Recap

Joseph found favor with both God and man, rising from slavery to become a powerful leader in Egypt, then redeeming his family and setting them up to become a great nation.

How to Find Jesus in This Story

Jesus can be found in the life of Joseph, who went from being a suffering servant to someone who forgave and saved his people. Jesus was also betrayed, but he rose to power and secured eternal life for all those who believe in him.

How to Apply This Lesson to Your Life

The story of Joseph teaches us the importance of forgiveness and resilience. Even when people choose to harm us, we must remain focused on being obedient to God's plan because he can use anything and everything for his ultimate good.

Part Three

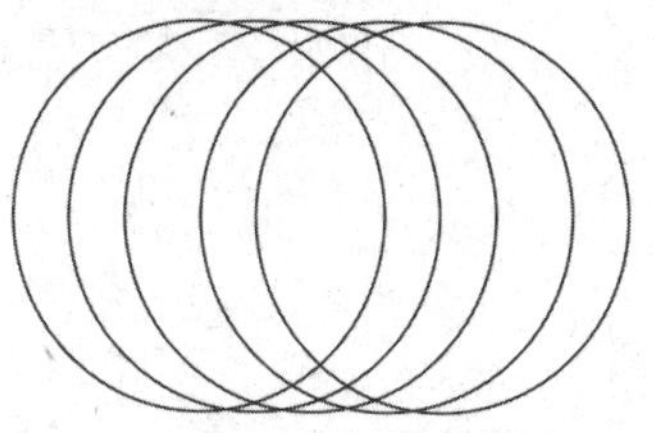

EXODUS AND THE PROMISED LAND

Chapter 11

The Early Life of Moses

Exodus 1–2

While the book of Genesis ends with Joseph's family moving to Goshen near Egypt to be taken care of by the Egyptian government, the book of Exodus begins with a very different scenario. Over the course of four hundred years, Jacob's group of relatives and in-laws grew from around seventy people into a people group with its own culture, customs, and of course, religion.

The pharaoh of Joseph's time had long since passed away, and the new pharaoh viewed the Israelites as a threat to the country's national security.

Afraid that there would soon be enough Israelites to conquer all of Egypt, Pharaoh enslaved them. He used the Israelites to make bricks, build cities, and be a source of free labor. Yet the enslaved Israelites continued having children, to the point where scholars estimate there may have been as many as three million of them. As far as Pharaoh was concerned, that was way too many.

He then commanded that all Israelite sons be thrown in the Nile River to drown. In his eyes, killing the next generation would stunt the people's exponential growth and give the Egyptian population time to catch up.

In the book of Exodus, we are introduced to a woman who had just given birth to a son, but she didn't obey Pharaoh's command to throw him in the Nile. In the Hebrew, Scripture says this boy she had was *tov*, which can be translated as "beautiful, robust, healthy, *good*." The last place we saw the word *tov* used in Scripture was in the Genesis story, when God created something and declared it was good.[1]

> "God created light and God saw that it was good [*tov*]."
> "God created animals and God saw that they were good [*tov*]."

So the text immediately indicates that this boy was different. He was something special, and God was going to do something unique through him.

The boy's mother hid him for three months until the risk became too great. She then placed him in a wicker basket—an "ark" or *tevah* in Hebrew. Up to this point in Scripture, the word *tevah* had only been used in connection to Noah's ark.[2]

> "Make yourself an ark [*tevah*] of gopher wood. Make rooms in the ark [*tevah*], and cover it with pitch inside and outside." (Genesis 6:14)

Something is happening here. The author was clearly trying to show the audience that this boy was going to bring in a new era for the Israelite people. The wicker basket was found by Pharaoh's daughter, who decided to raise the baby as her own son. The boy's big sister, Miriam, even managed to make sure that their mom was hired to nurse the baby.

As you've probably figured out by now, this boy's name was Moses. He rescued Israel from slavery and became one of the most revered and important figures in ancient history.

The story picks back up when Moses was around forty years old. He'd been raised in the lap of luxury by Pharaoh's own daughter, living a very different life from his fellow Hebrews, who were still slaving away on Egypt's building projects. One day Moses saw an Egyptian taskmaster savagely beating one of the Hebrews. Even though Moses was deeply removed from the Israelite culture at this point, he had great empathy for the man being beaten, so he stepped in to defend him and killed the Egyptian.

The next day, Moses went back to the same area and saw two Israelites fighting with each other. He stepped in again, trying to make peace between them, but they weren't interested. "What, are you going to kill me just like you killed the Egyptian?" one of them said.

Moses realized the cat was out of the bag, and he was on the hook for murder. So he fled his cushy palace life for a distant land called Midian.

When Moses arrived in Midian, he earned the favor of the local priest and even married the man's daughter Zipporah. After spending his whole life as royalty, Moses learned to make a living in the wilderness with a new family.

After what most scholars believe to be forty years or so, the pharaoh passed away. Then his son inherited the throne. The Israelites hoped things would improve under this new pharaoh, but their enslavement continued.

They cried out to God, and the Bible says: "God heard their groaning, and God remembered his covenant with Abraham, with Isaac, and with Jacob. God saw the Israelites, and God knew" (Exodus 2:24–25).

This was a turning point in the story. Things couldn't get much worse for the Israelites, but God had saved Moses for a reason. In the next chapter, we will look at the ways in which God used Moses to deliver them.

One-Sentence Recap

Pharaoh meant to harm the Israelites, but God was raising up a man named Moses to deliver them from slavery.

How to Find Jesus in This Story

Just as Moses had a heart for the hurting and helpless, we see the same passion against injustice through the life of Jesus, who called us to the same purpose.

How to Apply This Lesson to Your Life

When we see injustice happening around us, we should speak up and be a part of the change.

Chapter 12

The Exodus from Egypt

Exodus 3–15

After forty years of living as Egyptian royalty, Moses found a simple life as a shepherd in a land far away from home. He may have grown used to this existence, but he surely felt the loneliness and discomfort of being so far away from the land where he was raised.

One day as he was shepherding his flock for his father-in-law, he was out on Mount Horeb, which is also known as Mount Sinai, the "mountain of God." In the ancient world, mountains were thought of as high places that reached toward the heavens, so it was most common for God to meet with people on a mountain.

At this point in the story of the Bible, God hadn't spoken audibly to anybody since Jacob, a few hundred years earlier. As Moses was walking along the mountain, he came across a bush that was on fire. But the bush wasn't being consumed by the fire. Rather, it was continually burning.

As Moses watched the bush in amazement, God spoke to him from the fire. He said,

> "Moses! Moses!"
> And Moses said, "Here I am."

> "Do not come any closer," God said. "Take off your sandals, for the place where you are standing is holy ground . . . I am the God of your father, the God of Abraham, the God of Isaac and the God of Jacob . . . I have indeed seen the misery of my people in Egypt. I have heard them crying out because of their slave drivers, and I am concerned about their suffering. So I have come down to rescue them from the hand of the Egyptians and to bring them up out of that land into a good and spacious land, a land flowing with milk and honey . . . So now, go. I am sending you to Pharaoh to bring my people the Israelites out of Egypt." (Exodus 3:4–8, 10 NIV)

This is the moment we have been waiting for. We knew Moses was special. We knew he was going to be used by God at some point in his life. We just didn't know when. Now, nearly eighty years later, it's time.

God was calling Moses to help deliver the Israelites from Egypt.

Remember: Moses grew up in a polytheistic culture. As a boy in Egypt, he would have been taught to believe in many gods. But when he asked *this* God what his name was, God responded with, "I AM WHO I AM. This is what you are to say to the Israelites: 'I AM has sent me to you'" (Exodus 3:14 NIV).

I AM WHO I AM.

What a strange name, especially to us Westerners.

In Hebrew, the name is spelled *YHWH*, and the name can be translated as either "I am that I am," "I am who I am," or "I will be what I will be." God's name is a verb. He is always moving, doing, being.

YHWH.

Many modern-day English readers pronounce it as *Yahweh*. But the original readers had so much awe and respect for the name of God that they very rarely spoke the name out loud. Rather, whenever they came across the name when reading Scripture and in prayer, they would say *Adonai* ("the Lord") instead. And if they wanted to say his name in conversation, they would say *Hashem* ("the name").

God commanded Moses to go to Pharaoh and demand he let the Hebrews go. Moses obeyed, but Pharaoh basically laughed at Moses for even suggesting such a crazy thing. "Who does this YHWH, this God of the Hebrews, think he is?" he scoffed.

You see, in ancient Egyptian culture, the pharaoh was viewed as the physical manifestation of the sun god Ra, who was known as the chief god of the land. No other gods were superior to Ra, meaning no other God could tell a pharaoh what to do.

This interaction with Pharaoh was about to become a battle between YHWH and Pharaoh. Good and evil.

Who would prove to be the truly superior god?

Moses warned the pharaoh that God was going to bring ten different plagues to the people of Egypt. The plagues began. One after another.

Plague one: The Nile turned to blood.
Plague two: Frogs invaded the land.
Plague three: Insects attacked.
Plague four: Flies swarmed.
Plague five: Livestock died.
Plague six: Boils broke out.
Plague seven: Hail fell.
Plague eight: Locusts descended and destroyed.
Plague nine: Darkness fell across the land for three days, and the sun (Ra) was defeated.

Everything reached a climax with the tenth plague. God said he would kill the firstborn sons across all of Egypt, just as another pharaoh had done with the Hebrew babies eighty years prior.

To protect the Israelite boys from also being killed, God commanded the Israelites to sacrifice an unblemished lamb. They were to take the blood from the lamb and smear it all around their doorposts, so at night when the Lord went door to door, he would know to "pass over" the doors protected by the lamb's blood. Meanwhile, the Hebrews waited in their homes, observing this solemn event with a specially prepared meal.

This meal became known as Passover, and God went on to command the Israelites to observe it every year in remembrance of this moment. As Christians, we can see an incredible amount of symbolism here with Jesus as the Lamb of God and his blood protecting us as well.

The Israelites did as they were commanded. And that night, the Lord went into every house that wasn't protected by the blood of the lamb and killed the firstborn sons of Egypt.

This was the tipping point for Pharaoh, who allowed the Israelites to leave with their flocks and herds. The Egyptians even gave the Israelites all of their gold, silver, and clothing on the way out. It was finished. They were set free—all two million (or more!) of them at this point.

But Pharaoh and his officials quickly changed their minds after realizing what they had just done. They had lost their entire workforce in the blink of an eye. So they chased the Israelites, determined to take them captive again.

Moses and the Israelites had already made it to the Red Sea, but it appeared to be a dead end with the Egyptian army coming at them from behind. Doom seemed certain.

God told Moses to raise his staff over the Red Sea to split the waters from left to right. Moses did as he was commanded, and walls of water rose up on each side with dry ground in between, which allowed the Israelites to safely cross the sea. God performed a miracle for the Israelites by ushering them across the sea and protecting them.

As soon as the Israelites reached the other side, God caused the water to crash back down on Pharaoh's army, who had followed closely behind. No survivors remained.

Israel was now free.

But old ways die hard, as we will see in the next chapter.

One-Sentence Recap

God used Moses to bring his people to freedom from the evil oppression of Egypt.

How to Find Jesus in This Story

Jesus is symbolized as the Passover Lamb, and the Red Sea crossing symbolizes being born again through Christ.

How to Apply This Lesson to Your Life

The most important aspect of our faith is trusting in God's guidance even when it doesn't make sense to us. Though our circumstances may seem "impossible," when mixed with our faith and perseverance, God can turn them into something beautiful—in this case, a new beginning.

Chapter 13

Receiving the Law

Exodus 19–40; Leviticus 1–27

If you've ever tried a "Bible in a Year" reading plan, you most likely hit the second half of Exodus and Leviticus and thought to yourself, *What in the world am I reading?*

This is so boring.

Why would God make them do such crazy things?

What's with all of the sacrifices?

Do I need to follow these rules too?

This is also the part where you most likely stopped reading or at least skipped over until you got to something more interesting. We want stories, we want drama; we don't care about rules for skin diseases and whether God allows us to eat cheeseburgers, right?

People who have never read the Bible before assume the entire book is like the Law. They think it's full of rules specifying what you can and cannot do as a Christian. In reality, the laws make up a fairly small section compared to the rest of the text.

But why is it there at all?

After being miraculously set free from slavery, the Israelites were now in the desert on their way to the promised land. But they existed as a group of millions of slaves who didn't have their identity rooted in *anything.* God gave them a set of laws as a sort of national contract to teach the Israelites who he really was.

So Moses and the Israelites traveled through the wilderness to a place called Mount Sinai, and Moses met with God there. Up until then, God had only been in conversation with Moses. He hadn't spoken to the people as a whole yet. But now God told Moses to tell the Israelites: "You yourselves have seen what I did to Egypt, and how I carried you on eagles' wings and brought you to myself. Now if you obey me fully and keep my covenant, then out of all nations you will be my treasured possession. Although the whole earth is mine, you will be for me a kingdom of priests and a holy nation" (Exodus 19:4–6 NIV).

The Israelites had been bombarded with polytheistic culture for their entire lives. It was deep within them after serving in Egypt for hundreds of years. But kingdom culture (God's culture) was different from the one they'd known. So when God said he was calling his people to be holy, he was setting them apart from other nations. God's standard of perfection required separation from the unholy, because holiness cannot mix with anything that goes against its essence.

Life with this God was going to be different.

In our stories up until now, God had a relationship with individuals. He made a covenant with Abraham, then Isaac, then Jacob, who was renamed Israel. But this time, God made a covenant with a *group* of people: the Israelites as a whole. And he promised to bless them if they obeyed this covenant.

This was called the Mosaic covenant.

This covenant was a little different from those of the past. In the others, God promised to do certain things for his people, and they didn't have to do anything in return. In the Mosaic covenant, God gave his people a list of things to do to keep up their end of the deal.

God gave Moses the Ten Commandments, which are foundational for moral law throughout many parts of the world whether you believe in God or not. The Ten Commandments can be found in Exodus 20 and include

1. Have no other gods before the one true God.
2. Do not make idols.
3. Do not take the name of God in vain (by using his name in a way that dishonors him).
4. Remember the Sabbath day by keeping it holy.
5. Honor your father and your mother.
6. Do not murder.
7. Do not commit adultery.
8. Do not steal.
9. Do not bear false witness against your neighbor.
10. Do not covet.

God told the Israelites that if they obeyed these commands, they would be a representation of him to the rest of the surrounding nations. Remember the Abrahamic covenant that said Abraham's descendants would be a blessing to the rest of the world? This is a continuation of that promise.

In the past, the Israelites were passive participants in these covenants. Now God was involving them in the process as well. They needed some accountability for their actions.

God put rules and bumpers in place to help them along the way. One of these commands was to build a portable dwelling place for God, which the Hebrews called the tabernacle.

Since the very beginning in Eden, God wanted to be in relationship with his creation, walking and talking among humans, on earth. But after the fall, God could no longer be in that kind of proximity to people. God is so holy that he can't be in contact with any sort of sin—so he had to remove himself. But that wasn't good enough for God. He wanted to find a way. So God told Moses that he wanted the Israelites to build a tabernacle where he could reside among his people while they were in the desert.

God gave Moses detailed plans for what this tabernacle was to look like and how it was to be built in order to contain God's presence and protect sinful people from contaminating that holiness. It was to be a place where God could dwell among people, a place where heaven and earth could overlap again.

This is what the tabernacle setup looked like:

As you entered the tabernacle, the first area was called the outer court, which was where the altar of sacrifice was located. Here the priests would burn sacrifices to God on behalf of the people, all throughout the day. There was also a large pot of water that was blessed by the priests and meant to be used for ritual purposes.

The next place inside of the tabernacle was called the inner temple or the Holy Place. The only people allowed in this area were the priests who essentially represented all of Israel before God.

Inside the Holy Place were large menorah candles, a table with pita bread on it, and a smaller altar that looked like the one in the outer court, but this one burned incense instead of animals. The smoke represented the prayers of the people rising up to God.

The final, most important location within the tabernacle was called the holy of holies, where only the high priest was allowed to enter once a year on the Day of Atonement. The Day of Atonement was the day when all the sins of Israel would be forgiven. The holy of holies was the physical place of God's presence on earth.

To get into the holy of holies, the high priest would have to pass through a thick purple veil, which led into a room that held the ark of the covenant.

The ark was a gold-covered box with two angel statues on top of it. Inside of this ark were the stone tablets God had written the Ten Commandments on.

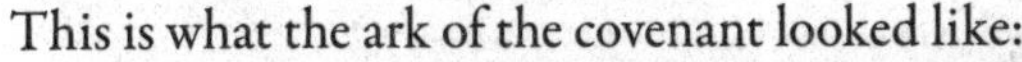

This is what the ark of the covenant looked like:

After describing what the tabernacle was supposed to look like, God gave the Israelites the rest of the law they needed to follow in order to be set apart as he had commanded them. This law was a list of 613 rules and regulations—a handbook on how to live a holy life.

The Israelites were now left with a choice, just like Adam and Eve. They could do life on their own, or they could follow God's laws and be the holy nation he had planned for them to be.

If they obeyed the laws, God's blessing would fall on them.

If they disobeyed, there would be consequences.

The issue was that this law had high standards. If the Israelites broke one of the 613 rules, they might as well be breaking all of them. So to compensate for their failures, a sacrificial system was attached to the law. If the Israelites messed up, they could sacrifice an animal and their sin would be covered, bringing them back into alignment with God.

As you can see, this was a *very* bloody covenant.

They had one bloody day after another. And it wasn't for a small group of people either. We're talking millions of people sinning every day, needing sacrifices for their redemption. The tabernacle's altar saw a constant flow of people (and blood). With each sacrifice, they would be covered for a day, but then they would sin again and be trapped in this cycle of sin and sacrifice.

No amount of bloodshed could wipe out sin completely.

And it wasn't meant to. The sacrificial system was only meant to be temporary.

For us, today, this seems like such a barbaric way of living. But it shows us how much we needed a Savior who could completely take away the sin of the world and put us in right relationship with God for eternity, not just one day. This is why Jesus' sacrifice on the cross is the cornerstone of our faith as Christians. He was the perfect, sinless, spotless Lamb of God, whose bloodshed covers all our sin if we place our trust in his sacrifice.

The Mosaic covenant was for a specific group of people, but it demonstrated to them *and* to us that we can't live up to God's standards of holiness on our own. Then and now, we are in need of a Savior.

One-Sentence Recap

The Israelites entered a new covenant with God to become a holy nation, and to represent God to the rest of the world.

How to Find Jesus in This Story

Jesus says he is the fulfillment of the law.

How to Apply This Lesson to Your Life

We should live in a state of gratitude for Jesus' sacrificial work on the cross.

Chapter 14

Shaping a Nation in the Wilderness

Numbers and Deuteronomy

The Israelites spent the next year at Mount Sinai as they became acquainted with the law and pulled a team together to build the tabernacle.

It was finally time for them to take over the promised land that God had told Abraham the Israelites would one day receive.

Before leaving, and since the people had grown into a major nation, Moses held a census to keep record of God's covenant promise. God's promises were coming to fruition.

Moses organized the Israelites into twelve tribes and taught them how they were to camp around the tabernacle. The tabernacle was to be situated in the center, with the Levites (the tribe in charge of worship at the tabernacle) surrounding it, and then the rest of the tribes in different, specific areas of the camp. If the people kept God at the center of their lives, they would always be protected and provided for, as seen in the layout God had commanded.

Whenever the cloud of God's presence raised up from the tabernacle, the tribes were to pack up their things and follow wherever it led them. At this point, they left Mount Sinai for the wilderness of Paran on the way to Canaan to receive the land.

But about halfway to the promised land, a tragic shift occurred.

Twelve spies (one from each tribe) were sent ahead into the promised land. Their job was to scout the location and determine what they would have to deal with in this new place.

Upon the spies' return, ten of them said, "There's no way we are going in there. We will surely die!" They were terrified of the armies they would have to defeat in order to claim the promised land as their own. The other two spies, Joshua and Caleb, came back with a much more positive report. They believed in the promise of God and knew he would take care of them as they entered the land.

It didn't matter what Caleb and Joshua said though. The people believed the frightening reports from the other spies and decided that entering the promised land wasn't an option. They lost their trust in God's plan. They even wished for a new leader who would take them back to Egypt—because even though they had been slaves there, at least they knew they were safe.

God didn't take their complaints lightly.

He got angry with the Israelites and told them their entire generation would spend the next forty years in the wilderness, wandering around until they died off. A journey that should have taken them a few days turned into a forty-year punishment, all because of their disobedience to the Lord's plan. Nobody in that generation would see the promised land. Their children would be the ones to enter instead.

God always keeps up his side of the covenant, but he also lets humans choose their fate. We can either do what he says and receive blessings, or we can do things on our own and let the consequences play out.

As the next generation grew up and the older generation began to die out, Moses took the people to the edge of the Jordan River, right outside the promised land. He renewed the covenant with this new, younger group. It was now up to them to grow closer to God, to be humble, to act in obedience, and to enjoy God's blessings in return.

If they obeyed God, he would save them from their enemies and take care of their needs.

If they disobeyed, the nation would fall apart.

They had a choice.

Just as they always did.

Moses went away to Mount Nebo, where he finally died in peace, after a long life of faithful service to and friendship with God. He left the Israelites in the hands of his successor, Joshua—one of the two spies who had trusted God's plan. Joshua would lead the people into the promised land, as we'll see in the next chapter.

One-Sentence Recap

Due to the Israelites' disobedience, they were forced to wander in the wilderness for forty years until the generation that left Egypt had died out, with only Joshua, Caleb, and the new generation being allowed to enter the promised land.

How to Find Jesus in This Story

Jesus can be viewed as our great Redeemer, who leads us into the ultimate promised land of eternal life.

How to Apply This Lesson to Your Life

If we trust in God's guidance and obey all he commands of us, we can be confident in knowing he will take care of our needs.

Chapter 15

Conquering the Promised Land

Joshua

The day finally arrived for the Israelites to take over the land that had been promised to Abraham hundreds of years before.

Joshua became a new leader, like Moses, at this point, taking charge of the people as a military commander and leading them into their destiny.

As they prepared to step into their promise, a river stood between them and their future, just as the Red Sea stood between the Israelites and their freedom decades before. The Jordan River wasn't huge by any means, but they had a lot of people and the water moved quickly—so it would take another miracle to get everyone across safely.

God told Joshua to have the priests lead the way, with the ark of the covenant in their hands.

When the priests placed their feet in the water, the river stopped flowing ahead of them. God opened up a space for the Israelites to pass through on dry ground . . . again. All of Israel passed to the other side, protected by God, providing the way for them to begin their takeover.

It was a miracle.

Joshua then chose twelve men, one from each tribe, to each take a large stone from the middle of the Jordan and place them together on the promised land side of the river. In the ancient world, people frequently collected and placed such stones as a way to remind themselves how God had moved. These memorial arrangements were called witness stones because every time someone noticed them, they would remember and speak about all God had done. In this case, when the Israelites' descendants saw these twelve stones next to the Jordan, they could ponder how God stopped the flow of the river so everyone could pass into the promised land.

Now that the Israelites were inside the promised land, it was time to take over. God commanded them to destroy everything inside Canaan: every city, every home, and every family, unless the people chose to join the Israelites in acknowledging the Lord as the one and only God.

This can be a pretty difficult story to read. Was God really calling the Hebrews to slaughter an entire land in his name? It's so easy to talk about the courage and bravery of Joshua and turn all of this into a cute lesson on Sunday morning. But when you think about what actually happened, the story is much harder to digest. God commanded them to partake in a violent, gory, R-rated task. After spending the last few chapters discussing how gracious and loving God is, this story can be pretty disruptive.

How could a God of love ask his people to be mass murderers?

Well, there comes a time when enough is enough. The Canaanites worshipped many different gods and chose to partner with the evil forces of the world, which led them deeper and deeper down the path to hell. Their culture was dark and demonic, and it was time for God to use his people to bring things back to order. To worship God meant to destroy the works of the devil, including ridding the world of physical evil.

If the Israelites obeyed God, he would bless them—and they would be able to show the other nations what the God of Israel was like. If they disobeyed and followed the ways of the Canaanites, curses would come their way. They had a choice.

And as we'll soon see, they chose to go against God.

The Bible tells us two contrasting stories about the Israelites embarking on their takeover: what happened when the Israelites followed God's plan, and what happened when they disobeyed.

The first city the Israelites conquered was called Jericho. And this story demonstrated the Israelites' obedience and the faithfulness of God.

Jericho was a major city. All trade went through this very wealthy hub along the crossroads of the world. God told the Israelites to march the ark of the covenant around the city walls once a day for six days straight. And on the seventh day, they were to walk around it seven times. Then, on the seventh time, God told them to blow a loud horn so the walls would come tumbling down on their own.

God was going to lead the way. The Israelites only had to obey, even when God's plan sounded crazy.

So they did just as God had commanded, and sure enough, the walls came crashing down and killed everyone inside. God had his hands all over the Israelites. All they needed to do was trust that his way was the right way.

The second story of the conquest was quite different.

Amid the Battle of Ai, one of the Israelites sinned against God by taking some of the goods from the land for himself instead of destroying them as God had commanded. The sin of one man led to punishment for the whole group.

After this one man kept a few spoils of war, the Israelites went into their second battle and were defeated. They quickly saw what would happen if God wasn't fighting on their side. Once they discovered the one soldier's sin and repented, God led them to victory yet again.

The message of these two stories is clear: If the Israelites obeyed God, they would be given victory over the land. If they disobeyed, he would let them fight for themselves and eventually lose. Obedience is an easy concept, but it is hard to actually live out.

The Israelites remained loyal to God for the time being and were led to victory again and again across the land, conquering every place God had planned for them. Their many successes testified to his faithfulness.

The Lord renewed his covenant with the Israelites, promising to keep fighting for them as long as they were obedient to the law. Once the Hebrews had conquered the promised land, they had control of the world's most influential area—and God could begin his plan of renewal through his people.

In the next chapter, we'll see how quickly things took a turn for the worse.

One-Sentence Recap

God led the Israelites into the promised land, then guided them to victory over the Canaanites and a full conquering of the land.

How to Find Jesus in This Story

Just as Joshua led the Israelites into the promised land, Jesus leads us into our ultimate promised land of eternal life thanks to his victory over sin.

How to Apply This Lesson to Your Life

If we are obedient to the Lord's commands, he will lead the way and fight our spiritual battles for us.

Part Four

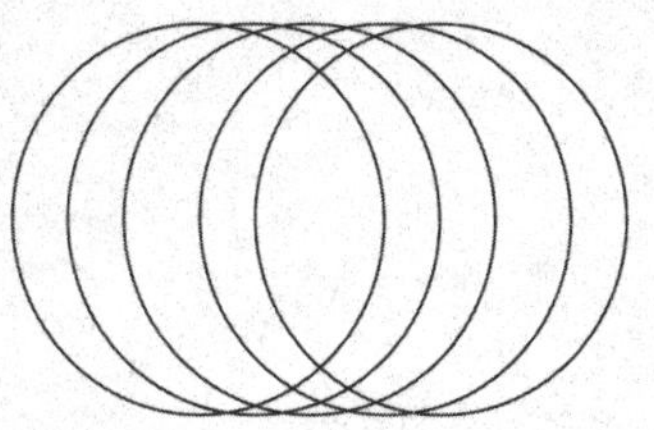

KINGDOMS AND PROPHETS

Chapter 16

Judges

The book of Judges is one of the hardest sections of Scripture to read. Just like the book of Joshua, Judges is violent and disturbing. Some people wouldn't believe you if you told them such stories could be found in the Bible. They're *that* messed up.

The Israelites went into the promised land just as God commanded them—ravaging some of the Canaanite towns, killing every person and animal in sight, burning down the villages, and claiming the land for themselves. But they didn't destroy everything. The Israelites were quick to disobey God, and they allowed some of the Canaanites to live. This was the exact opposite of what God had commanded them to do.

Why was this a big deal?

Because God didn't want his people, the Israelites, to adopt the cultural practices of the Canaanites. Today we wonder, *What possibly could've been so bad about the Canaanites that God didn't want them to live anymore?*

The Canaanites' chief creator god was named El. According to Canaanite mythology, everything came from El. El had a wife named Asherah who was the fertility goddess of both the land and humanity. So if someone wanted a successful harvest season and blessings on their offspring, they would worship Asherah.

In Canaanite mythology, Asherah and El gave birth to Baal. (Remember that name, because you'll come across it many times as you study Scripture.) Over time, in Canaanite culture, El became less important, and Baal became the main god. He was a fertility god like his mother, bringing blessings to the land and humanity.

So Baal took his mother, Asherah, as his mistress goddess (yeah, I know, it's weird), and they became the two most worshipped deities in the Near East. And Israel succumbed to the pressure to worship these gods instead of their God, who had brought them out of Egypt.

And how did the Canaanites worship Baal and Asherah? Mass orgies with temple prostitutes, many of whom were likely sex slaves.

Not only that, but the idols to another god, Molech, had furnaces inside of them. The idols had outstretched arms, with hands burning red-hot from the heat of the fire inside. During these ceremonies, the women worshippers would take their firstborn children to the priests, who would then place the babies into the burning hands of Molech as an act of worship and devotion. They were willing to burn their children alive so their god would bless them in return.

How sick and twisted this was compared to what God had planned for his people. Orgies with sex slaves and child sacrifice were two rituals God didn't want his people associated with.

The Israelites didn't listen though. They began to blend their worship between both God and Baal. But when something clean mixes with something unclean, the whole thing becomes unclean. God handed the Israelites over to their hearts' desires, which led them down the path toward destruction.

But God, out of his patience, was always there for his people whenever they were ready to return. So the book of Judges introduces a series of cycles that the Israelites experienced.

The Israelites would do evil in the sight of God.
Then God would allow their enemies to oppress them.
Again the Israelites would cry out to God for help.
Then God would raise up a judge to deliver them and bring them to a time of peace.

Over and over again.

Now, Old Testament judges weren't legal experts like you and I think of them. The Bible calls them judges, but they were more like divinely appointed heroes. They were often political or military leaders who could bring the people to victory.

This cycle of sin took place twelve different times for the Israelites, six of which are described in depth. The stories involving judges like Othniel, Ehud, Deborah, Gideon, Jephthah, and Samson are often ugly and full of violence, rape, and murder. They illustrate how quickly Israel fell into chaos when they stopped obeying God.

Even though God commanded the Israelites to be holy and set apart, very little difference could be found between the Israelites and their neighbors. When they fell, they fell hard.

One phrase is repeated in the book of Judges: "In those days there was no king in Israel; everyone did what was right in his own eyes" (17:6; 21:25 NASB). God wanted them to do what was right in his eyes, but just like Adam and Eve back in the garden of Eden, the Israelites chose differently.

But God is patient.

This repeated reminder in the book of Judges placed an emphasis on hope. All this happened when the Israelites had "no king" and chose to do things on their own—meaning they needed something (or someone) to get them back in line: a king who would take them there!

We'll learn about the first Israelite kings in the next chapter and how they began to reform the people for God.

One-Sentence Recap

The Israelites chose to do things their own way, which perpetuated a cycle of evil, oppression, and repentance, followed by deliverance by various judges raised up by God himself.

How to Find Jesus in This Story

Jesus can be seen as the ultimate Judge who delivers people from sin and spiritual oppression through his sacrifice on the cross.

How to Apply This Lesson to Your Life

When we try to do things on our own, it is easy to fall away from God's plan. We must remember to seek his guidance and trust that his ways are greater than ours, even when we think we are making the best decisions.

Chapter 17

The Kings and the Temple

1 and 2 Samuel

Israel was in great need of a king, someone who could lead the people in the ways of God. There is a small, beautiful story in the book of Ruth, right after the book of Judges, that hints at a man named David being the king the people needed.

In 1 and 2 Samuel we meet three main characters: Samuel, Saul, and David.

Samuel: The Last Judge and First Prophet

In 1 Samuel we learn about a man named Samuel who became God's mouthpiece.

The Israelites didn't want to be led by judges anymore. They went to Samuel and asked if God would provide them with a king like the other nations had. They wanted to fit in, and every time they tried to fit in, their efforts came back around to bite them instead.

But God agreed to their request for a king, provided they understood how it might cost them more than they realized. He wanted them to know what would happen ahead of time, so God said,

> This is what the king who will reign over you will claim as his rights: He will take your sons and make them serve with his chariots and horses, and they will run in front of his chariots. Some he will assign to be commanders of thousands and commanders of fifties, and others to plow his ground and reap his harvest, and still others to make weapons of war and equipment for his chariots. He will take your daughters to be perfumers and cooks and bakers. He will take the best of your fields and vineyards and olive groves and give them to his attendants. He will take a tenth of your grain and of your vintage and give it to his officials and attendants. Your male and female servants and the best of your cattle and donkeys he will take for his own use. He will take a tenth of your flocks, and you yourselves will become his slaves. When that day comes, you will cry out for relief from the king you have chosen, but the LORD will not answer you in that day. (1 Samuel 8:11–18 NIV)

Sounds like a pretty awful deal, huh?

But the people said, "We still want a king so we can be like all the other nations!"

So God gave them what they wanted, and the people of Israel entered the time period of the kings.

Saul: The First King of Israel

For their first king, the Israelites chose a man named Saul who was tall, dark, and handsome. He looked the part of a strong leader, comparable to the other kings in the area. Saul was their man.

And sure enough, Saul started off as a great king for Israel. He led them into battles against the Philistines and Moabites and Ammonites and Edomites and Amalekites and was victorious in all of them. Everyone loved Saul. And everyone loved his son Jonathan, who was also a great leader and would eventually take over the throne (or so the people thought).

Saul was proud of Jonathan. He would make sure everyone knew how strong and powerful his son was, as Jonathan led them to victory right alongside his father. But over time, Saul's pride became his downfall. He started disobeying God and began to lose his grip on reality. The Bible says an unclean spirit came on him. This man who had started out as such a promising leader was corrupted by power and became wicked. Samuel himself abandoned Saul in search of another king who would be a better fit for Israel.

David: From Shepherd to King

Saul remained king for the time being, but Samuel went out on his own, led by God, in search of Saul's replacement. Israel needed a king who was humble and faithful to the Lord.

The Lord said to Samuel, "Fill your horn with oil and be on your way; I am sending you to Jesse of Bethlehem. I have chosen one of his sons to be king" (1 Samuel 16:1 NIV).

So Samuel arrived at Jesse's home and asked to meet his sons. Jesse introduced him to his oldest sons, who were all great warriors and who, like Saul, looked the part of a king. They had everything they needed on the outside, but God was looking at the inside.

Samuel said, "Do you have any other sons? None of these is the one I'm looking for."

"Well, I do have one more, but he's just a young shepherd boy," said Jesse.

When David walked in, the Lord immediately let Samuel know this was the one to be seated on the throne once Saul died. Samuel anointed David with oil, and the Holy Spirit was upon him from that day forward.

So Samuel had anointed another person as king, though Saul was still on the throne. David was young, and it wasn't time for him to step into his calling yet. The Lord often does that. He calls us to something special, but it can be years before the calling actually comes to fruition.

Later on, David ended up at the front lines of a battle and defeated a giant named Goliath with nothing but a slingshot. As a shepherd, he'd learned how to fight the animals that threatened his flock—so how different could a giant be?

In that moment, Saul saw something special in David. Of course, Saul didn't know that God planned for David to take his place as king. All he knew was that David was a formidable warrior who was popular with the people, so Saul treated him well. David also became fast friends with Saul's son Jonathan. But as time went on, David became a little *too* popular in the eyes of Saul.

As David won battle after battle, the people would sing out, "Saul killed thousands, but David killed *tens* of thousands" (1 Samuel 18:7, emphasis added). Everyone loved David. But as that mockery rang in Saul's ears, jealousy began to consume him. He began plotting how to kill David.

So David fled to the wilderness to hide from Saul and his troops. He became an outlaw, living on the run from Saul and the other authorities, while also building up his own army of strong, capable people who were also living on the wrong side of the law. It was during this time that David started writing a lot of what we now know as the Psalms.

A few years later, Saul died an awful death at the hands of his enemies. Just as God had planned, David took over the throne. It was David's time to shine as the Lord's anointed one. David was a different type of king.

He was a king of humility and compassion instead of jealousy and anger. David loved the Lord and knew that his every success was a result of the Lord's presence in his life.

The first thing David did as king was go up to the city of Jerusalem and defeat the Jebusites who lived there. He claimed Jerusalem as Israel's capital, moved the ark of the covenant into Jerusalem, and established the city not only as the political center but also as the religious center of the nation. David asked God if he could build a temple in Jerusalem, but God said it wasn't the right time for such a thing. Still, God created a covenant with David (the Davidic covenant, which we discussed earlier), where God promised that one day he would send a Messiah, a king through David's royal line, to instate an eternal kingdom—that kingdom being God's.

This was the greatest time of Israel's history. David's leadership was wise and good, and the country was back on track with God's plan.

David wasn't perfect though. He had an affair with a woman named Bathsheba and eventually married her, but not before plotting to have her husband, Uriah, assassinated in battle. David and Bathsheba had a son named Solomon, who played a major role in the development of Israel.

The second half of David's life wasn't easy. He made mistake after mistake, and the consequences were great—but the Bible says he remained a man after God's own heart (1 Samuel 13:14; Acts 13:22) and continued to repent whenever he messed up. Jewish people today still pray for one of King David's descendants, the Messiah, to come and take over the throne once again, to lead them to political victory and bring God's kingdom to the world. As Christians, we believe this Messiah was and is Jesus.

When King David was on the verge of death, he handed the reins of the kingdom over to his son Solomon.

Solomon began as an incredible king. His name in Hebrew means "peace," which is exactly what the nation experienced under his kingship.

One night, the Lord appeared to Solomon in a vision and said, "Ask for whatever you want me to give you."

"I don't know how to be a king," Solomon replied. "So I would like wisdom to govern the people and know the difference between right and wrong."

The Lord said, "Since you asked for wisdom, I'll not only give you wisdom but also everything else you didn't ask for—all the wealth, honor, and power you could imagine" (1 Kings 3:5–14, paraphrased).

As king, Solomon built a temple—a larger, more beautiful, and permanent version of the tabernacle that the Israelites had been using since the days of Moses.

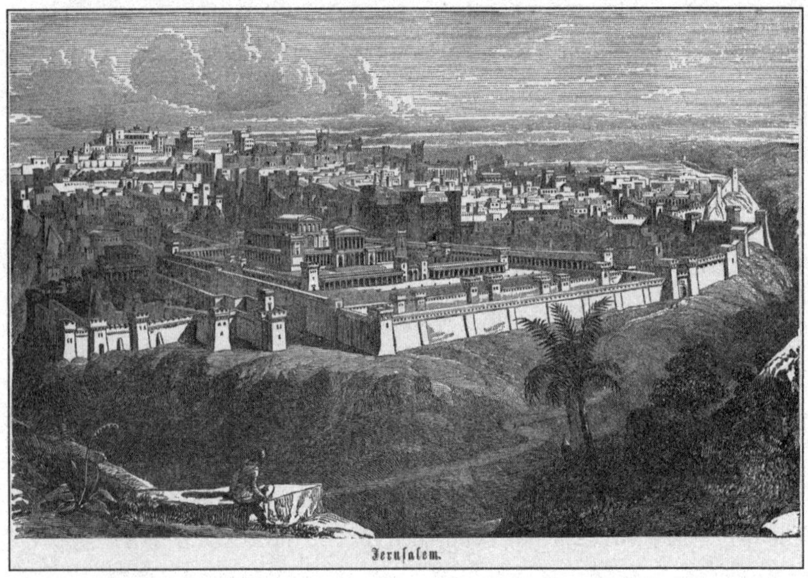

Jerusalem.

The temple was built on the top of Mount Moriah, which is the same location where Abraham was tested by God in sacrificing Isaac. This was such a holy and important place for the Israelites because God showed up there in miraculous ways. This temple was a remarkable feat of ancient engineering, but its completion also kicked off a very rocky future for

Israel's kingdom. The books of Kings and Chronicles detail the nation's heights of glory—when Israel's kings and people walked closely with God—all the way down to the depths of despair as they fell away and, eventually, split into two separate kingdoms, which we'll learn about in the next chapter.

One-Sentence Recap

A monarchy was established in Israel beginning with the reigns of Saul, David, and Solomon.

How to Find Jesus in This Story

Jesus is the ultimate King and Messiah, the fulfillment of God's covenantal promises to David of the eternal kingdom.

How to Apply This Lesson to Your Life

We should put our trust and hope in God every day, being obedient to the calling he has placed on each of our lives.

Chapter 18

The Divided Kingdom

1 and 2 Kings; 1 and 2 Chronicles

The golden age of Israel came to a close with the passing of Solomon and the continuation of the kingdom. This is all covered in 1 and 2 Kings and 1 and 2 Chronicles.

The books of Kings tell the history of the Jewish people under their various kings, with emphasis on the bad ones. Almost every single king the books talk about is awful, except for only a few good ones found in the southern kingdom of Judah. The books were written shortly after their events took place, similar to a newspaper account of what was going on. The stories evaluated Israel from a political point of view.

The books of Chronicles were written hundreds of years later, once the Israelites returned from exile (which we'll learn about shortly). So these books provided readers with historical accounts to inspire them for the future. Chronicles emphasized the few good kings Judah had and evaluated their history from a religious perspective more so than a political one.

The Division of the Kingdom

When Solomon died, his son Rehoboam took the throne. And just like his father, he wanted more power. He gained it by increasing the taxes and making some of the Israelites work under him.

But it wasn't good for morale. That's for sure.

In response, the people revolted. Then ten of the tribes of Israel appointed a new king named Jeroboam to lead them instead. Remember what happens when people appoint their own leader outside of God's will? Yeah, it doesn't turn out well.

The ten tribes in the North decided to split off from the two tribes in the South and form their own nation.

The North continued to call themselves Israel.
The South called themselves Judah.

The Northern Kingdom (Israel)

The biggest issue with the North was that they no longer had access to Jerusalem, the temple, or the royal bloodline of David. God had said that one day he would send a descendant of David to the throne of Israel, to bring revival among the people. And since they didn't have access to the bloodline of David, they couldn't appoint his descendant as king. The true line of David was still in Judah.

Jeroboam chose Samaria as the capital city of Israel, and he placed two golden cows in the cities Bethel and Dan as a way for the Israelites to worship God instead of going to Jerusalem. He thought he could keep the people in his territory by giving them a place to worship, but this act did far more harm than good. God's presence was only in the temple in Jerusalem, and any other sort of idol worship was prohibited—so the cows led the Israelites down a slippery slope. They ended up worshipping both their God and the Canaanite gods Baal and Asherah.

Every single king on the throne in the North (Israel) brought the people further and further away from God's plan. Out of all twenty kings that reigned, none of them was considered righteous in the eyes of God.

So in 722 BC God sent the Assyrian Empire, one of the major world powers of the time, to invade Israel and take them away from their land. The Assyrians destroyed everything in sight. Many people were killed, others were taken into slavery, cities were demolished, and the evil that the Israelites brought upon themselves was given to them in return. It was a devastating time for the Jewish people, as the invasion wiped out all ten of the Northern tribes for good.

The Southern Kingdom (Judah)

The Southern Kingdom had a different experience. They had a major advantage over the North because of their access to Jerusalem, the temple, and the bloodline of David.

Whereas Israel had no good kings whatsoever, Judah was more of a roller coaster between good and bad kings. Out of their twenty kings and one queen, eight were considered good kings, and two of these were *really* good kings: Hezekiah and Josiah.

What made a good king good was his focus on righteousness, his desire to rid the land of idolatry, and his desire to bring the people of Judah back into right relationship with God. If the people obeyed God's commands, he would take care of them. And we see that promise playing out in how the Southern Kingdom survived 140 years longer than the Northern Kingdom.

Even still, the Lord's anger burned for the past mistakes and how the people had abandoned the law. They remained divided in their allegiance, trying to worship Baal and Asherah at the same time. They lasted longer, but it was only a matter of time before their sins caught up to them as well.

So in 586 BC, 140 years after the fall of Israel to Assyria, Judah fell too. God sent the world power Babylon, led by King Nebuchadnezzar, to ravage Jerusalem. Babylon destroyed the temple and sent a large portion of the people (including the bloodline of David) into exile.

This can be such a confusing moment in Scripture because God seemed to have given up on his people. The story might have ended here. But with so many pages left in the Old Testament, we know something else must've happened. And it did.

During the time of the Northern and Southern kings, God sent prophet after prophet to speak on his behalf, trying to convince the people to return to the ways of God. These prophets were meant to bring hope for the future. We'll learn more about these prophets in the next chapter.

One-Sentence Recap

The kingdom of Israel was divided into two conflicting nations, Israel in the North and Judah in the South, but both ended up falling to other world powers.

How to Find Jesus in This Story

Jesus is the ultimate King who will one day unite all his people.

How to Apply This Lesson to Your Life

The more we choose to focus our attention on righteousness and obedience to God's Word, the more we will be in line with his will and provision. The opposite is also true: If we try to mix worldly ways with God's ways, we are walking ourselves toward destruction.

Chapter 19

Major and Minor Prophets

Isaiah, Jeremiah, Lamentations, Ezekiel, Daniel, Hosea, Joel, Amos, Obadiah, Jonah, Micah, Nahum, Habakkuk, Zephaniah, Haggai, Zechariah, and Malachi

When you hear the word *prophet,* what comes to mind? Someone who knows things about you that nobody else does? Someone like a fortune teller, maybe?

Well, the prophets of the Old Testament were a strange bunch. Society had a hard time accepting them, especially prior to the exiles we talked about in the last chapter. The prophets were pushed to the side and written off as oddballs. But their role was incredibly important.

The prophets of the Old Testament were the mouthpieces of God, speaking on his behalf to the people. A prophet told their audience how God was feeling about their current situation and what God planned to do in the future, whether good or bad.

They were God's messengers, speaking with God's authority. The prophet was the middleman.

What Are the Prophetic Books in the Bible?

Seventeen books in our English Bible are considered to be "prophetic books," and they are all lumped together in the second half of the Old Testament.

The prophetic books are split into two main categories: major prophets and minor prophets (or "The Twelve" as they are called in the Hebrew Bible).

Major Prophets	Minor Prophets
• Isaiah • Jeremiah (and his Lamentations) • Ezekial • Daniel	• Hosea • Joel • Amos • Obadiah • Jonah • Micah • Nahum • Habakkuk • Zephaniah • Haggai • Zechariah • Malachi

By no means are these books divided into categories based on importance. The major prophets are just longer books. The minor prophets are shorter.

What Did the Prophets Write About?

Most people who read through the Bible for the first time struggle with this section because it's full of strange visions, commands, warnings of destruction, and promises of blessing. On the surface, the books don't seem to have any relevance to our lives today . . . until you learn how to study them.

The prophetic books focused on four main topics:

1. **Judgment and Redemption.** The Israelites were constantly breaking their covenant with God. So the prophets spoke about the judgment that would come upon them as punishment for their disobedience if they didn't repent. They also spoke about God's promise of redemption and hope for future salvation.
2. **Restoring Relationship with God.** The prophets urged their audience to renew the covenant with God and return to the place of a proper relationship with him, set apart to be a holy nation.
3. **Messianic Prophecies.** Many of the prophets spoke about a Messiah, a Savior, who would be sent to the people of Israel to bring justice, peace, and salvation. The Messiah would initiate a true golden era for the people and positively impact every nation.
4. **New Covenant and Future Hope.** The prophets spoke of a day when all would be made right in the world. Even though the Israelites were being punished, God would restore them and remain faithful to his promises.

The core directive in all of these books is to return to God. Should the people repent of their evil ways and turn back to God, they would be saved from the Lord's judgment and enjoy his promised blessings.

These books also look forward to the promised Messiah. In the very beginning of the Bible, at the time of the fall, God promised to one day send a person, a savior, who would help humanity restore their relationship with God. As the storyline progressed, we learned about Abraham and Moses and King David, and how God made the same promise to all of them as well.

The promise had been dragged out for centuries, continuing even further with the prophets.

This long-awaited Savior was known as the Messiah, which is Hebrew for "the anointed one." Our Bibles also translate the Greek word as "the Christ." So when you read "Jesus Christ," the word "Christ" isn't his last name. It's actually his title:

Jesus the Christ.
Jesus the Messiah.
Jesus the Savior.
Jesus the Anointed One.

I encourage you to dig in and read through the prophetic books at least once. The following overviews don't do them justice, but they might give you a sense of what the books are about.

Summaries of the Major Prophets

Isaiah

Isaiah warned about the coming judgment on Judah, along with a handful of other nations. He also gave the people a renewed sense of hope by talking about the promised Messiah who would bring peace and salvation to the people of Israel.

Jeremiah

Jeremiah is known as the "weeping prophet" because of the grief he felt toward the people of Israel. He warned them of the coming Babylonian invasion and exile, but nobody believed him. Like Isaiah, he also spoke about a new covenant that God would make with his people in the future.

Lamentations

Lamentations is Jeremiah's book of poetry, as he wept over the destruction of Jerusalem and the temple at the hand of Babylon.

Ezekiel

Ezekiel prophesied to the people of Israel while in Babylonian exile. He used a bunch of symbolic visions and actions to express God's judgment upon them, but he also described their eventual restoration. He even gave them hope for a new, restored temple.

Daniel

Daniel was taken into captivity in Babylon, and God helped him get promoted to a high rank in the Babylonian Empire. He prophesied about the coming eternal kingdom and the rule of the Messiah.

Summaries of the Minor Prophets

Hosea

Hosea's life and marriage to a sex worker acted as an illustration of the relationship between God and unfaithful Israel. It demonstrated God's mercy and called the people of Israel to repentance.

Joel

Joel warned of a locust plague that would symbolize God's judgment toward his people. He also foretold the outpouring of God's Spirit on all people, which we will see happening in the New Testament.

Amos

Amos was a shepherd and prophet in the Southern Kingdom who warned the Northern Kingdom of the judgment coming their way. He spoke mainly about their social injustices and their need for repentance.

Obadiah

Obadiah delivered a short but powerful prophecy against a neighboring nation, Edom, for their actions against Judah. They, too, would be punished.

Jonah

Jonah was sent to the city of Nineveh in Assyria to call the entire city to repent. Because Nineveh was full of enemies, Jonah tried to run away from his assignment—but God interceded with a storm and a giant fish. Jonah eventually preached to the Ninevites, who repented of their evil ways. In this story, God's mercy is on full display.

Micah

Micah warned of judgment against both Israel and Judah for their sins. He also prophesied of a future ruler who would be born in Bethlehem and bring peace to the nations.

Nahum

Nahum predicted the final destruction of Nineveh to offer comfort to Judah. Even though they repented during the time of Jonah, they ended up backsliding and turned away from God again.

Habakkuk

Habakkuk questioned why God was allowing so much injustice in Judah, but he discovered that God was going to use Babylon to bring judgment on the people of Judah for their sins.

Zephaniah

Zephaniah warned of the coming "Day of the Lord," a time of judgment for Judah and the surrounding nations. This fulfillment began with the Babylonian exile and will be completed at the end of time. He also spoke of a future restoration of God's people.

Haggai

Haggai encouraged the returned exiles to continue rebuilding the temple in Jerusalem and to put God first in their lives.

Zechariah

Similar to Haggai, Zechariah had a series of visions and prophecies focused on rebuilding the temple, all of which offered the Israelites hope for the future. He included multiple prophecies about the coming Messiah and how God's kingdom would reign supreme.

Malachi

Malachi prophesied to the Israelites who returned from exile, calling them again to repentance for their evil ways. They were right back to where they started before exile.

One-Sentence Recap

The prophets of the Old Testament frequently spoke about judgment, redemption, the Messiah, and a time in the future when God would usher in a new covenant with his people.

How to Find Jesus in This Story

As Christians we believe Jesus was the long-awaited Messiah and that his life was a fulfillment of hundreds of messianic prophecies.

How to Apply This Lesson to Your Life

Now that we know where the title messiah came from, we can choose to accept Jesus as the fulfillment of these prophecies.

Part Five

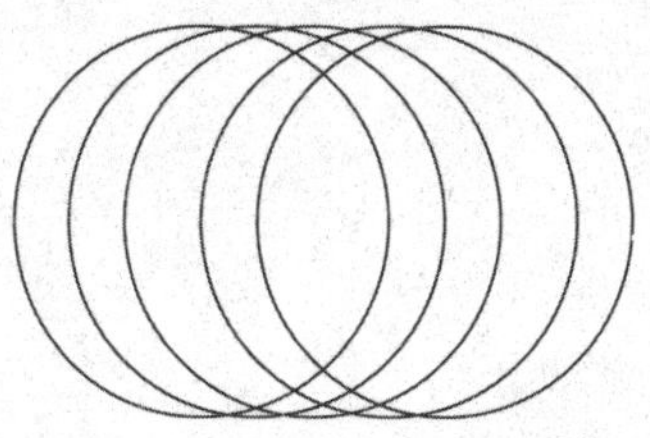

WISDOM AND POETRY

Chapter 20

The Psalms

When you're angry, read the Psalms.

When you're depressed, read the Psalms.

When you're happy, read the Psalms.

When you're grieving, read the Psalms.

When you're full of gratitude, read the Psalms.

When you have no idea what to say to God but you're feeling all of these different emotions and some days are high and some days are low and you just aren't sure anymore . . . spend time soaking up the words of the Psalms.

Why?
Because Jesus did.

As a Jewish man in the first century, Jesus would have thought of the Psalms as his prayer book.

Psalms consists of 150 poems and songs, from multiple authors, written over the course of hundreds of years. King David wrote seventy-three of them, Solomon wrote a few, Moses wrote one, the Sons of Korah and Asaph wrote others, and about one-third of them are anonymous.

In the Hebrew Bible, the name of this book is "Praises," because no matter what you are going through in life, you always have a reason to praise God.

Think of the Psalms as songs the Israelites would have known by heart. The priests at the temple sang them all day long, and everyone who came there to worship would join in. The temple was their connection to God, and the Psalms gave them words to express whatever they were going through.

Imagine how the Israelites felt when Babylon took over the city of Jerusalem, burned down the temple, and dragged them all into exile. They no longer had a way of connecting with God. They were now in a new city, feeling lost and hurt. It's in this setting that a group of scribes began to compile these 150 psalms into the book of Psalms we know today.

The Psalms were meant to be memorized, sung, and meditated upon, and they gave the people hope for the future. God was going to pull them out of exile. They just didn't know when.

Three Main Types of Psalms

Many different types of psalms can be found throughout the book, but the three main types are praise and thanksgiving psalms, lament psalms, and wisdom psalms.

Praise and Thanksgiving

Praise and thanksgiving psalms are self-explanatory. They revere God and thank him for who he is and what he did for the Israelites.

No matter how good or bad life is, we can always find a reason to praise God—so this type of psalm reflects on the never-ending goodness of God.

An example of a praise and thanksgiving psalm is Psalm 100:

> Shout for joy to the LORD, all the earth.
> Worship the LORD with gladness;
> come before him with joyful songs.
> Know that the LORD is God.
> It is he who made us, and we are his;
> we are his people, the sheep of his pasture.
> Enter his gates with thanksgiving
> and his courts with praise;
> give thanks to him and praise his name.
> For the LORD is good and his love endures forever;
> his faithfulness continues through all generations. (NIV)

Lament

A lament is a cry for help. So in a lament psalm, the author is crying out to God, asking the question *why*.

Why did you leave us?

Why are we going through this?

Why, why, why?

Lament psalms outnumber the other types, and they teach us how to express emotions that we may not feel comfortable talking about at church. The Israelites invited God into every emotion they felt, even when those emotions weren't comfortable or convenient, and he was always gracious to provide answers to them. God wanted the Israelites to be honest with him so they could experience life together—even the most painful moments. He wants the same thing from us.

An example of a lament psalm is Psalm 130:

> Out of the depths I cry to you, Lord;
>   Lord, hear my voice.
> Let your ears be attentive
>   to my cry for mercy.
> If you, Lord, kept a record of sins,
>   Lord, who could stand?
> But with you there is forgiveness,
>   so that we can, with reverence, serve you.
> I wait for the Lord, my whole being waits,
>   and in his word I put my hope.
> I wait for the Lord
>   more than watchmen wait for the morning,
>   more than watchmen wait for the morning.
> Israel, put your hope in the Lord,
>   for with the Lord is unfailing love
>   and with him is full redemption.
> He himself will redeem Israel
>   from all their sins. (NIV)

Wisdom

Wisdom psalms are slightly different from the last two types. They were intended to teach something, to show the audience what it meant to live righteously according to God's standards. Unlike the praise and lament psalms, these psalms were more instructional in nature than emotional.

An example of a wisdom psalm is Psalm 1:

> Blessed is the one
>   who does not walk in step with the wicked
> or stand in the way that sinners take
>   or sit in the company of mockers
> but whose delight is in the law of the Lord,
>   and who meditates on his law day and night.

That person is like a tree planted by streams of water,
    which yields its fruit in season
and whose leaf does not wither—
    whatever they do prospers.
Not so the wicked!
    They are like chaff
    that the wind blows away.
Therefore the wicked will not stand in the judgment,
    nor sinners in the assembly of the righteous.
For the LORD watches over the way of the righteous,
    but the way of the wicked leads to destruction. (NIV)

How to Read the Book of Psalms Today

As Christians we are no longer stuck in Babylonian exile. But we are still waiting for the return of Jesus, anticipating a time when we will be with him for good. The process has started, but it isn't yet complete. So today we can use the book of Psalms as a way to worship God. We don't study this book like we would other sections of the Bible.

The Psalms are beautiful and were designed to bring us closer to God in a heartfelt way—focusing our attention on knowing him rather than knowing more *about* him. They are intended to guide our emotions and are meant to be reflected upon, both individually and corporately. I encourage you to spend time reading a psalm every day, learning the ways our ancestors interacted with God.

One-Sentence Recap

The book of Psalms is a collection of poems and songs that help guide our emotions toward alignment with God.

How to Find Jesus in This Story

The Psalms contain multiple messianic prophecies about Jesus and show how he was the fulfillment of the promises found within the book.

How to Apply This Lesson to Your Life

The Psalms can be used as a guide for worship, prayer, and reflection, helping us express our emotions to God.

Chapter 21

Wisdom Literature

Psalms, Proverbs, Ecclesiastes, Song of Songs, and Job

The Bible features many different genres of writing. As we read through it, we should be reading each genre in its unique way. One of the literary genres is called wisdom literature. The Old Testament has five books that fit into this category: Psalms, Proverbs, Ecclesiastes, Song of Songs, and Job.

Wisdom for the Jewish people was not just about what one thought. It was about how one lived. It was about character and behavior. To have wisdom was to have right thinking, which led to right action.

As we grow in wisdom, we grow closer to God and his plan for our lives. The Bible's wisdom literature can help us do just that.

Proverbs

The book of Proverbs is all about developing character in righteousness and living up to God's standards. And as we read these proverbs, we will become wiser ourselves.

What is a proverb?
A proverb is a short and simple phrase that offers wisdom.

One of the recurring themes of Proverbs is fearing the Lord. Solomon says, "The fear of the LORD is the beginning of knowledge, but fools despise wisdom and instruction" (Proverbs 1:7 NIV).

The word *fear*, in this sense, means having awe and reverence for God. It's less about being scared than about having the utmost respect, acknowledging that God controls everything, and placing him above all else. Doing so humbles us, and we become reliant on God and his ways. Fearing God is about trusting that he knows better than we do.

Here are some examples of proverbs:

> "Trust in the LORD with all your heart
> and lean not on your own understanding;
> in all your ways submit to him,
> and he will make your paths straight" (3:5–6 NIV).

> "Above all else, guard your heart,
> for everything you do flows from it" (4:23 NIV).

> "Better to live in a desert
> than with a quarrelsome and nagging wife" (21:19 NIV).

> "The generous will themselves be blessed,
> for they share their food with the poor" (22:9 NIV).

If you choose the way of wisdom, you will live a very good life. And vice versa.

Ecclesiastes

"Everything is meaningless."

That's not the most encouraging concept for a book, especially a book of the Bible, but that seems to be the focus of Ecclesiastes if you just read through it quickly. It's a very strange, depressing book. In fact, a lot of people over the years have questioned its place within the canon of Scripture.

But when you understand its underlying theme, you can better understand its importance.

The book of Ecclesiastes pursues the question, What is the meaning of life?

The text begins by introducing us to a man called "the Teacher" (or "the Preacher," as some Bibles translate it), who had a goal of finding the answer to life's greatest question. He realized that nothing was more discouraging than getting to the end of life and deciding it was all pointless.

Life is like a vapor, he wrote. One minute you're here, and the next minute you're gone with nothing to show for it.

The book follows the Teacher as he tried "everything under the sun" to find meaning. He wanted to see if anything on earth would bring him a true sense of purpose.

Money. Pleasure. Knowledge. Work.

All the same routes we pursue today to find our own purpose. It worked as well for him as it does for us. Nothing seemed to satisfy him. Hence his conclusion that "everything is meaningless."

This book would be extremely discouraging if it ended there. But it doesn't.

The book ends by echoing what was written in Proverbs: "Now all has been heard; here is the conclusion of the matter: Fear God and keep his commandments, for this is the duty of all mankind. For God will bring every deed into judgment, including every hidden thing, whether it is good or evil" (Ecclesiastes 12:13–14 NIV).

So what is the meaning of life?
To fear God and keep his commandments.

Song of Songs

If I were to tell you that one book of the Bible was full of sexual metaphors, would you believe me?

Well, it's true.

The book is called Song of Songs—or Song of Solomon, as some Bible translations call it.

But the book isn't a song like we think of songs today. It's a collection of love poems. Song of Songs isn't discourse or narrative; it's poetry, so we should read it like poetry.

You've most likely heard verses from Song of Songs quoted at weddings. Things like

> "My love is mine and I am his" (2:16).

> "You have captured my heart, my sister, my bride.
> You have captured my heart with one glance of your eyes,
> with one jewel of your necklace" (4:9).
>
> "I found the one I love" (3:4).

If you keep reading, you'll run into verses that say,

> "Your breasts are like two fawns,
> twins of a gazelle, that feed among the lilies" (4:5).
>
> "Blow on my garden,
> and spread the fragrance of its spices.
> Let my love come to his garden
> and eat its choicest fruits" (4:16).
>
> "Your stature is like a palm tree;
> your breasts are clusters of fruit.
> I said, 'I will climb the palm tree
> and take hold of its fruit.'
> May your breasts be like clusters of grapes,
> and the fragrance of your breath like apricots.
> Your mouth is like fine wine" (7:7–9).

Talk about some wild poetry! And this is found in the Bible?!

Song of Songs explores the relationship between a man and a woman who were madly in love and engaged to be married, and the sexual tension that stretched between the two. It's not the most comfortable book to study in a church setting.

So what's really going on here? Why in the world is this collection of poems in the Bible?

Well, love and sex are meant to be gifts from God.

Job

Job is the quintessential book on suffering.

We all want to know the answer to the question, Why do bad things happen to good people?

The book of Job explores that question, but it doesn't give the answer we'd prefer.

The book begins by telling us about Job. He was a blameless and upright man who feared God and hated evil. Job was blessed beyond belief with a beautiful family and a massive farm. The Bible even says he "was the greatest man among all the people of the east" (1:3).

The story then transitions to a courtroom setting in heaven where God was consulting with his "divine council," one of whom was Satan.

God asked Satan if he had tried any of his evil ways toward Job, because God was so confident in Job's righteousness that he believed Job would never fall away. God almost seemed to be betting that Job wouldn't give in, no matter how many bad things happened to him.

Satan accepted the challenge.

A few verses later we learn about Job's life falling apart. His animals were stolen, his servants were killed, his house was destroyed, and his children all died.

Job lost everything.

Yet Job did not blame God.

The story switches to a poetic style of writing and introduces us to three of Job's friends: Eliphaz, Bildad, and Zophar. They approached Job's situation as any respectable person in the East would have: by grieving with their friend in silence.

After seven days of silence, Job began to speak, which opened up the conversation for the others to share some of their thoughts about what was happening to Job. They also gave their theories about *why* it was happening.

Why did God allow him to suffer?

Why was this happening to Job?

And was God just in his actions?

Job's friends thought he *must* have committed some sort of major sin to have invited this kind of punishment and plague upon him and his family.

When Job's friends had said their piece, God entered in a whirlwind, ready to humble Job for demanding an answer from God. Who did Job think he was to expect an answer from the God of the universe? So God spoke to Job in the most epic, poetic speech, full of rhetorical questions, demonstrating his own power. He said things like,

> "Where were you when I laid the foundations of the earth?
> Tell me, if you know so much.
> Who determined its dimensions
> and stretched out the surveying line?" (38:4–5 NLT)

> "Have you ever commanded the morning to appear
> and caused the dawn to rise in the east?
> Have you made daylight spread to the ends of the earth,
> to bring an end to the night's wickedness?" (38:12–13 NLT)

> "Can you shout to the clouds
> and make it rain?

> Can you make lightning appear
> and cause it to strike as you direct?" (38:34–35 NLT)

Chapter after chapter, God presented his case.

> "Do you still want to argue with the Almighty?
> You are God's critic, but do you have the answers?" (40:2 NLT)

"Then Job replied to the LORD,

> 'I am nothing—how could I ever find the answers?
> I will cover my mouth with my hand.
> I have said too much already.
> I have nothing more to say.'" (40:3–5 NLT)

The story ends with Job having all his fortunes restored, twice as great as before. The Bible says, "the LORD blessed Job in the second half of his life even more than in the beginning" (42:12 NLT).

God doesn't shy away from our questions. He sits with us in our pain and allows us to process it. He just wants us to trust him even when our circumstances don't make sense. There is so much more going on around us that we cannot even comprehend.

So why do bad things happen to good people?

I don't know. Nobody does.

When we understand that the universe doesn't revolve around us but that we are part of God's plan, the weight and pressure can come off our shoulders and be placed on God. Our confidence comes from knowing that he works everything out for our good.

One-Sentence Recap

Wisdom literature shows how God shows up in the major questions of life, in suffering and celebration and even in love and sexuality.

How to Find Jesus in This Story

Much of wisdom literature asks where God is and what our purpose is—questions that would be answered by the coming of Jesus.

How to Apply This Lesson to Your Life

We must learn that true wisdom begins with the fear of the Lord.

Part Six

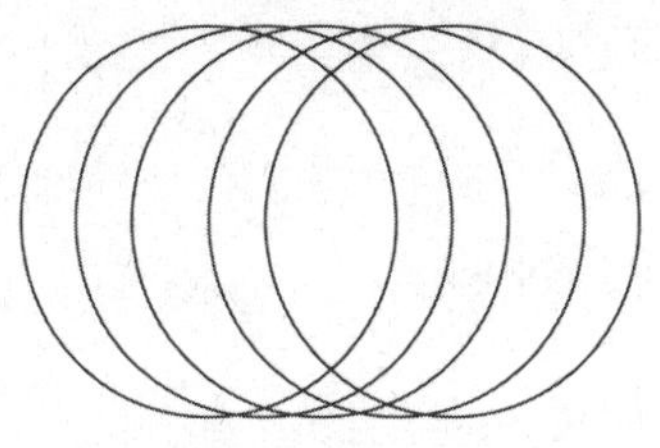

EXILE AND RESTORATION

Chapter 22

The Babylonian Exile

2 Kings, 2 Chronicles, Ezra, Jeremiah, Lamentations, Daniel

One of the most important themes of the Old Testament is the exile of the Israelites. I've already mentioned it briefly, but what happened during that time?

Early in the Genesis story, God promised Abraham, Isaac, and Jacob that he would give them special land. The Israelites settled in the promised land, and it seemed like God's promise was fulfilled.

But then God took that land away from them. What was happening?

Well, the major world powers in the Middle East during the seventh century BC were Egypt, Babylon, and Assyria. Those were the big dogs.

When King Nebuchadnezzar led Babylon, his goal was to take over the known world. After winning a gruesome battle against Egypt in 605 BC, he became the literal king of the world. Nebuchadnezzar brought his army through the region of Judah (remember, the Northern Kingdom of Israel was taken into exile by Assyria, and the Southern Kingdom of Judah was all that was left), demanding that they accept his position as king. Over the next twenty years, Nebuchadnezzar laid siege three times on Judah. Finally, with the third one in 587–586 BC, he claimed victory.

Judah was ransacked.

The walls surrounding the city were destroyed.

Tens of thousands of people were killed.

Thousands more were taken into captivity.

And the temple, where God's presence resided, was in rubble.

This was a tragedy. Everything the people of Judah had built for hundreds of years was destroyed in a matter of days.

As the people of Judah were led away from their land, they were devastated to see how the temple had been demolished. How confusing that must have been—to have believed that God had promised them the land in the first place, and that he had promised to reside among them, only for him to . . . seemingly disappear?

They felt broken.

Abandoned.

Betrayed.

Defeated.

But they had brought it upon themselves.

Their downfall didn't happen overnight. They had been disobeying the

Lord's commands and adopting the ways of their neighbors ever since entering the promised land. God was faithful to his promises through the prophets, warning the people that they would one day be in exile if they didn't turn their lives around.

God was sovereign and faithful to his word.

But remember, the prophets didn't just warn of future exile. They also gave the people hope for the future. One day, they proclaimed, all would be restored. God's people would be led back to their land to rebuild the temple.

This was only a temporary time for the Israelites.

This period of exile didn't involve slave labor like the Israelites had experienced in Egypt. Sure, they were under the rule of Babylon, but they were subjected to more than just manual work. The Israelites were forced to adopt the ways of the Babylonian culture. Nebuchadnezzar was a clever ruler. He gave the nations he conquered a certain amount of freedom as a way of keeping them in line. The Israelites were largely allowed to go about their ways—working, building, creating families, and enjoying life under their new leadership.

God spoke to the Israelites through the prophet Jeremiah, saying, "Build houses and settle down; plant gardens and eat what they produce. Marry and have sons and daughters; find wives for your sons and give your daughters in marriage, so that they too may have sons and daughters. Increase in number there; do not decrease. Also, seek the peace and prosperity of the city to which I have carried you into exile. Pray to the LORD for it, because if it prospers, you too will prosper" (Jeremiah 29:4–7 NIV).

But even though circumstances may not have seemed so bad for the exiles on the outside, their identity as God's people was being attacked the most. They no longer had a temple for worshipping God, and they couldn't offer sacrifices as they had been commanded by the law.

They had two options:

1. Adopt the ways of Babylon and accept the Babylonian gods as their own.
2. Stay faithful to YHWH and focus on the hope of an eventual return.

This spurred a movement of sorts, as the exile motivated some Israelites to spend their time reading the Law and growing closer to God in any way possible. The people were proud of their heritage and believed God would be faithful to his promises. This exile lasted for seventy years, and many people who were born in Babylon had no recollection of what the temple looked like or even what it meant to be their own nation.

Just as God sent prophets to Israel *prior* to the exile, he also sent a few prophets *during* exile to encourage them in their faith. Jeremiah prophesied, saying,

> "The days are coming," declares the LORD,
> "when I will make a new covenant
> with the people of Israel
> and with the people of Judah.
> It will not be like the covenant
> I made with their ancestors
> when I took them by the hand
> to lead them out of Egypt,
> because they broke my covenant,
> though I was a husband to them,"
> declares the LORD.
> "This is the covenant I will make with the people of Israel
> after that time," declares the LORD.
> "I will put my law in their minds
> and write it on their hearts.
> I will be their God,
> and they will be my people.

> No longer will they teach their neighbor,
> or say to one another, 'Know the LORD,'
> because they will all know me,
> from the least of them to the greatest,"
> declares the LORD.
> "For I will forgive their wickedness
> and will remember their sins no more." (Jeremiah 31:31–34 NIV)

Whenever the Israelites lost hope, the prophets would encourage them to press on because a new covenant was on the horizon.

When the Israelites forgot their identity, the prophets would remind them who God called them to be.

When the Israelites would question God's intent, the prophets would explain the heart behind his actions.

They offered comfort and the promise of future restoration.

They promised a future king—the Messiah.

Yes, this was a time of punishment for the Israelites, but it was *restorative punishment.* They came out on the other side a stronger and more resilient people.

Would they remain faithful to God?

Would their identity be restored?

Would they stay strong or bow down to the Babylonian Empire?

The thing is, kingdoms that aren't based around God will eventually fall—something we'll learn more about in the next chapter.

One-Sentence Recap

The Babylonian exile was an emotional roller coaster for the Jewish people, as their temple was destroyed and they were taken into captivity; but they also grew stronger through their understanding of God's sovereignty and the hope of restoration.

How to Find Jesus in This Story

The prophets of exile spoke of a coming Messiah who would bring the ultimate restoration and create a new covenant between God and his people.

How to Apply This Lesson to Your Life

No matter how difficult our situation, we need to trust in God's sovereignty and remain hopeful that he is working behind the scenes. We should also be encouraged to pursue our faith even more diligently whenever outside pressures increase.

Chapter 23

Returning and Rebuilding

Ezra and Nehemiah

The exile was a confusing time for the Israelites.

In 539 BC, during the seventy years of exile, the great nations of Persia and Media joined forces and conquered the Babylonians under the rule of a man named King Cyrus. King Cyrus was a polytheist who acknowledged that Babylon had taken over different people groups, all of whom worshipped different gods that would need to be appeased.

So to ensure he would receive the blessings of each nation's gods, Cyrus allowed the people to return to their hometowns to rebuild their religions, provided they made sure to pray for his kingdom. Sounds like a pretty good deal, if you ask me.

The time had finally come. The Israelites were being brought back into the land with all the resources necessary to rebuild. It seemed too good to be true. In three waves, large groups of Israelites left exile and returned to the promised land to rebuild their lives, their culture, and their nation. They also rebuilt the temple in 516 BC, though it was not nearly as magnificent as the one Solomon had built years earlier.

When the Second Temple was completed, the Israelites threw a huge party to celebrate being back in relationship with God. But their expectations didn't match reality. They thought the occasion would be like what their ancestors had experienced at the dedication ceremony of the tabernacle and First Temple, when God's spirit came down to reside with his people (Leviticus 9; 1 Kings 8).

But it didn't happen that way. His spirit didn't come.

The temple remained empty. It didn't make sense. The Israelites had done everything that they were supposed to, but where was God? Why hadn't he come?

Here we are introduced to two people who would lead the second and third return to Jerusalem: Ezra and Nehemiah. Each had a specific task.

Ezra was like a new Moses for the Israelites. He would renew the covenant between God and the Hebrews. And Ezra would lead a group of nearly two thousand Levites and priests back to Jerusalem in 458 BC, sixty years after the Second Temple was completed. We skip over so much time when we read the Bible, but let that time gap sink in. This was sixty years after the completion of the Second Temple.

Ezra was a devout Jew who was zealous for Scripture. The Bible was everything to him. Not only did Ezra study Hebrew Scripture, but he also lived it out and inspired others to do the same.

He was the perfect man for the job.

We are then introduced to a man named Nehemiah.

While Ezra loved Scripture, Nehemiah loved prayer and was reliable.

If Ezra was the new Moses, Nehemiah was the new Joshua.

Both types of people were necessary for building the new community of God's people in Jerusalem.

Nehemiah was the cupbearer for the king of Persia, which meant his job was to taste the king's wine to make sure it wasn't poisoned. It was a very important job because the king had to have full faith and trust that the cupbearer wasn't out to kill him. Nehemiah and the king would have known each other very well.

The king knew Nehemiah to be a very joyful man, but Nehemiah got word that things weren't going very well for the Israelites back in Jerusalem. He learned that since the walls had been destroyed, the people of Israel were vulnerable to attacks from their neighbors. Upon hearing this, Nehemiah became discouraged, and the king could tell something was off. Nehemiah explained the situation to the king and asked if he could go up to Jerusalem to help build the walls for the people.

King Artaxerxes agreed and even offered to provide Nehemiah the resources necessary to get the job done.

So in 444 BC, Nehemiah headed out to Jerusalem with a group of people who would help rebuild the walls around the city and make it secure for the Israelites.

Things were really looking good for the Israelites at this point. They were motivated in their faith and ready to go back to the ways of their ancestors. Ezra had them all gather inside the city walls, and from early in the morning until the afternoon, he would read the Law to them for hours—the scrolls of Genesis and Exodus and Leviticus and Numbers and Deuteronomy.

This was the first time many of these returned exiles had ever heard the entire story of their ancestors, and they began to weep upon realizing how far they had strayed from God's original plan. It was a rebirth of a nation.

Life was going to be different now. God had pulled them out of exile and given them a fresh start. It was a day of joy, not sorrow.

So the Israelites threw a huge party, celebrating God's provision in their lives and reflecting on how God had provided for their ancestors in the same way he was providing for them now.

The temple was rebuilt. The covenant was renewed. They were back in the land God had promised them. All was right in the world.

The Messiah *should* arrive any day now, right?

One-Sentence Recap

Ezra and Nehemiah were sent to Jerusalem to help rebuild the Jewish community through spiritual reform, covenant renewal, and the restoration of Jerusalem's walls, but things didn't go according to plan.

How to Find Jesus in This Story

As close as God's people were to ushering in the messianic era, their hearts weren't ready yet. Jesus would soon arrive to bring the people's hearts back to God and fully restore that relationship.

How to Apply This Lesson to Your Life

This story should inspire us to build the foundation of our lives on God's principles, obeying the Word and trusting his guidance when opposition comes our way.

Chapter 24

"The Silent Years"

The final book of our Old Testament ends with a warning by the prophet Malachi around 430 BC. He said, "See, I will send the prophet Elijah to you before that great and dreadful day of the LORD comes. He will turn the hearts of the parents to their children, and the hearts of the children to their parents; or else I will come and strike the land with total destruction" (Malachi 4:5–6 NIV).

And then the prophecy ends. That's it. That's the last thing spoken to the people of Israel for over four hundred years.

It's easy for us to flip the page from the last words of Malachi right to the birth of Jesus in the New Testament, but that one-page flip represents four hundred years of history for the Jews. Some people call this the "intertestamental period" or the "four hundred years of silence" because there was no prophetic word from God during this time. All the people had to hold on to were the prophecies from the past.

Was God really silent?

Or was he just preparing the way for the coming Messiah?

To address this question, let's pause for a quick history lesson. If we know what took place beyond the Bible's historical record over this four-hundred-year period, we can better understand what was happening in

Jerusalem and the surrounding areas—because even though God wasn't speaking to the people through a prophet, a lot was taking place in the lives of the Jews.

Greek Rule (336–166 BC)

Alexander the Great rose to power in Greece in 336 BC, and as his influence grew in the area, so did his power. He expanded his kingdom outside of Greece and into other parts of the world, eventually stretching all the way to India. Alexander the Great's empire became so dominant that the East officially became Greek.

Everyone under Greek rule had to adapt to Hellenistic culture, including the Jews. They learned the language, they developed new passions, they learned Greek philosophy (like that of Socrates and Aristotle), and they adopted new gods as their own.

Alexander the Great was kind to the Jews during his reign, allowing them to practice their religion as they pleased. But that didn't last for too long. Alexander died in 323 BC, resulting in the division of the Greek Empire and a two-hundred-year battle for control of Jerusalem.

Persecution of the Jews rose to an all-time high at this point.

But many of the Jews were resilient. Their passion for God's law only increased. They knew persecution sometimes comes with the territory for those who obey God.

The Maccabean Revolt and Hasmonean Dynasty (167–63 BC)

When enemies of the Jewish people desecrated the temple by sacrificing unclean animals on the altar, the Jewish people decided enough was enough. A man named Judas Maccabaeus and his family and friends banded together to violently revolt against the foreign forces and were successful at driving them out of the land in Judea.

So in 164 BC the Jews reclaimed Jerusalem, tore down pagan altars, and rededicated the temple to God.

For the first time in hundreds of years, the Jewish nation was free from outside powers—but that didn't mean everything was easy for them. They were still in a constant battle with the Syrians in the North who were vying for power. But the Jews remained strong.

Roman Rule (63 BC–New Testament Period)

While the Jews were doing their best to maintain control of the land, Rome was growing in influence around the East. Internally, the Jews began to fight among themselves, leading to an all-out civil war. To solve this disorder, the Jews asked Rome to control them and act as a mediator between their factions. Israel became part of the Roman Empire.

The Jewish people were back to square one: under the control of another empire. The Jews could still do their own thing within their borders, but the ultimate ruler with the final say was now Rome.

A wealthy Jewish man named Antipater offered his help to the Romans, so Julius Caesar made him governor of Judea. He didn't last long, though, as he was quickly poisoned by one of his rivals. His son Herod became the new king of the Jews. Herod's fame and influence grew across the land as he became very wealthy, eventually receiving the nickname Herod the Great.

Herod died in 4 BC, leaving the rule of Judea in the hands of his three sons, Herod Archelaus, Herod Antipas, and Philip.

Jewish Culture

Even though life seemed pretty unstable for the Jewish people, a lot of great things were taking place that allowed for the advancement of the gospel later on. For example,

- The majority of the East spoke Koine Greek, making it possible for the gospel message to spread all through the land without translators. The Old Testament was even translated into Greek—a translation called the Septuagint—and most of the Old Testament quotes you will find in the New Testament came from the Septuagint.
- New roads were built to connect much of the known world, including major trade routes throughout the Middle East and into Western Europe.
- As long as people pledged their allegiance to the Roman Empire, they had religious freedom and could practice their faith as they pleased. This doesn't mean they weren't oppressed. They definitely were. But their faith wasn't stripped from them.
- Synagogues were built throughout the land as places of worship, education, and community.

God was moving in the background, putting the pieces in place for the coming of the Messiah.

Sects of Judaism

As all of this was happening, Judaism split into many different groups, kind of like the denominations we have in the church today. Their foundation was the same, but what the groups chose to focus their attention on varied drastically. Three of the main sects of Judaism at the time were the Pharisees, Sadducees, and Essenes.

Pharisees

The Pharisees focused on the law. They emphasized the priestly laws because of what Moses said in Exodus 19:5–6: "Now if you obey me fully and keep my covenant, then out of all nations you will be my treasured possession. Although the whole earth is mine, you will be for me a kingdom of priests and a holy nation" (NIV). The Pharisees built their entire beliefs around this understanding that all of Israel was meant to be a "kingdom of priests and a holy nation."

Sadducees

The other main group at the time was the Sadducees, who were in direct competition with the Pharisees. They didn't like each other. As a Jew, you chose to align with either the Pharisees or the Sadducees, so when Jesus entered the scene, people would ask him questions to try to figure out who he was aligned with.

The Sadducees were aligned with local leadership. They helped dictate the way Israel was run politically and tried to influence how the Jewish people were treated.

Essenes

The Essenes were Jewish people who isolated themselves from Greek influence. They did such a good job of isolating themselves that we don't know a ton about them today, but we do know that they withdrew from mainstream culture, like we might picture a monk doing. The Essenes' focus was on preparing themselves for the arrival of the messianic era. If you've ever heard of the Dead Sea Scrolls that were found in Qumran, you might also know that one of the main Essene communities likely collected those scrolls.

The Apocrypha

Even though the church often calls the intertestamental period "the silent years," that doesn't mean nothing new was written *about* God.

Tons of books were written by various Jewish people during this time frame. The importance of these books has been debated for centuries, because while the early church did not believe the books to be divinely inspired literature, many today believe the books can be very useful for understanding the culture Jesus was born into.

We call this time period the "Second Temple period" and its writings the "Second Temple writings." Different Jewish authors were writing a lot of books—twelve of which became very popular within the early church and were categorized as the Apocrypha.

The twelve main books of the Apocrypha are Tobit; Judith; Additions to Esther; Wisdom of Solomon; Sirach; Baruch; Letter of Jeremiah; Additions to Daniel; 1, 2, and 3 Maccabees; and 1 Esdras.

Some different denominational groupings of the Apocrypha also include Psalm 151, the Odes, 2 Esdras, 4 Maccabees, Jubilees, the book of Enoch, and others, but those aren't considered part of the main twelve.

The word *Apocrypha* comes from the Greek word meaning "hidden things," and if your Bible includes the Apocrypha, you'll usually find this collection of books placed between the Old and New Testaments.

Since these books were written during the silent years, there is a major debate between the Protestant Church and the Catholic Church and Eastern Orthodoxy on whether they should be included in our Bibles today.

The Hebrew Bible does not include these books as canon, but they were very popular books during Jesus' day and as the early church expanded.

So that leads us to this question: Should we consider the Apocrypha a part of Scripture?

It all depends on which Christian tradition you subscribe to. In the

Protestant tradition of the West, the books are read for historical information during the Second Temple period but are not considered divinely inspired. In other areas of the Catholic and Orthodox Church, most of the books are believed to be inspired by God. The answer is based on the tradition you claim as your own.

I'd recommend reading them at least once with an open mind and a respectful attitude toward other Christians in the faith. You will agree with some stuff you read, and you'll disagree with some things as well. That's okay. The goal is to grow in our knowledge of God and to understand the history of our people.

One-Sentence Recap

The four hundred years of silence was a time of continual political turnover in Judea, but each change prepared the world for the arrival of the Messiah.

How to Find Jesus in This Story

During this time frame, the expectation of the Messiah was increasing because of the many prophetic writings that foreshadowed his coming. Further, the widespread establishment of Greek and Roman culture eventually made the rapid spread of the gospel message possible.

How to Apply This Lesson to Your Life

We need to recognize that times of waiting or silence from God can be times of preparation and growth, so long as we trust that God is moving behind the scenes.

Part Seven

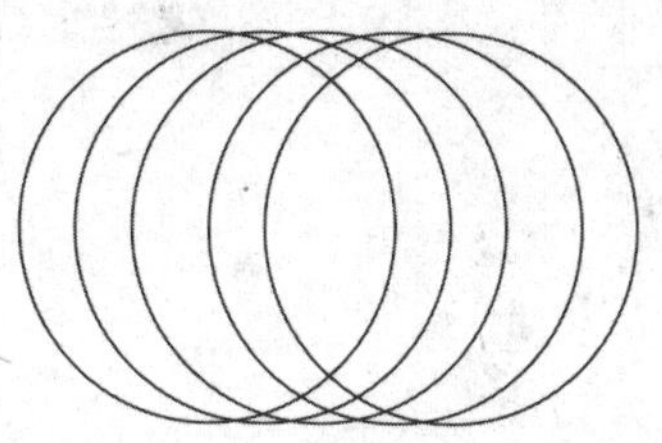

JESUS THE MESSIAH

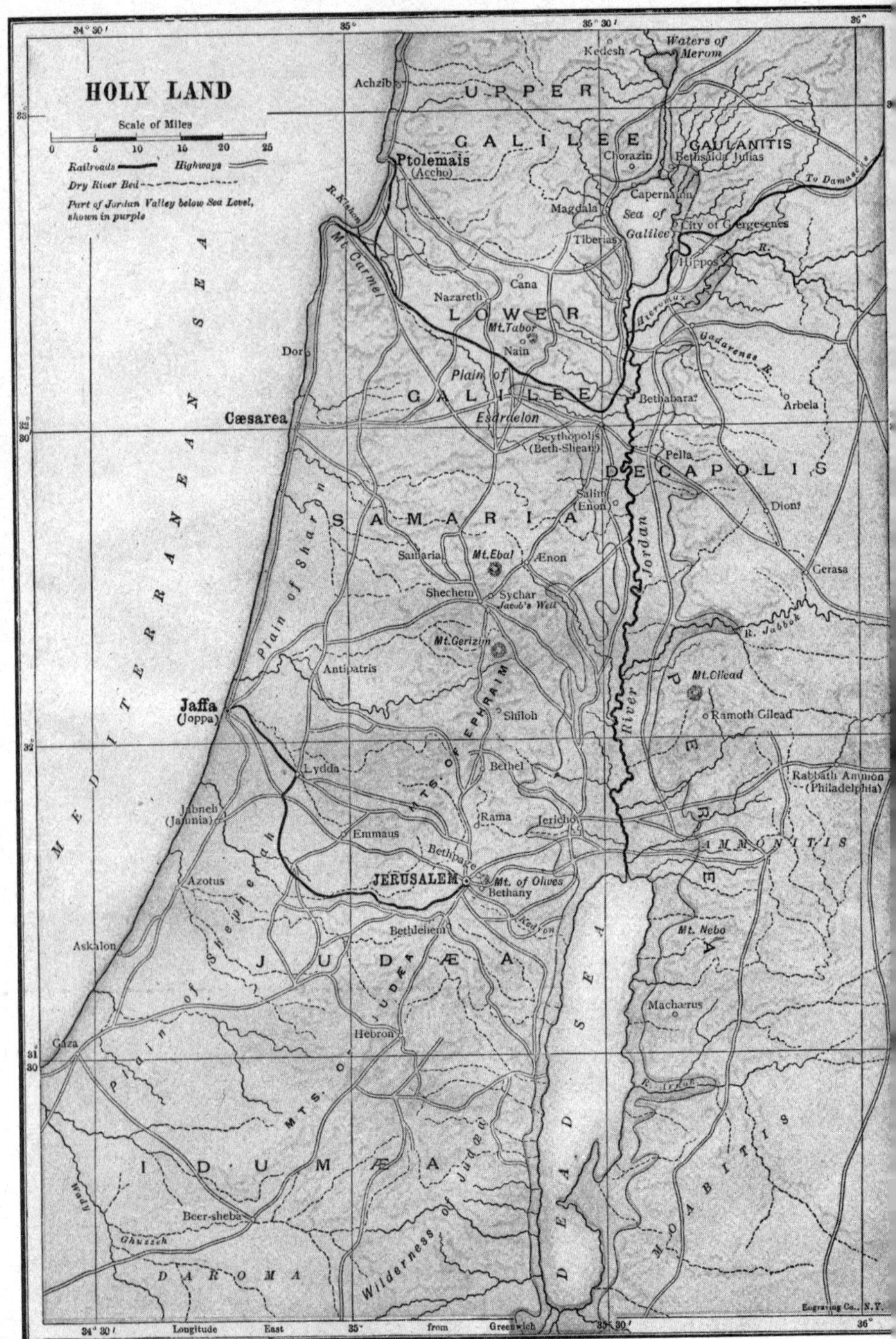
HOLY LAND
Scale of Miles
0 5 10 15 20 25
Railroads
Highways
Dry River Bed
Part of Jordan Valley below Sea Level, shown in purple
MEDITERRANEAN SEA
UPPER GALILEE
LOWER GALILEE
GAULANITIS
DECAPOLIS
SAMARIA
JUDÆA
IDUMÆA
PERÆA
AMMONITIS
MOABITIS
DAROMA
DEAD SEA
Waters of Merom
Kedesh
Achzib
Ptolemais
(Accho)
Chorazin
Bethsaida Julias
Capernaum
Magdala
Sea of Galilee
Tiberias
City of Gergesenes
Hippos
To Damascus
R. Kishon
Mt. Carmel
Cana
Nazareth
Mt. Tabor
Nain
Dor
Plain of Esdraelon
Hieromax
Gadarenes R.
Bethabara
Arbela
Cæsarea
Scythopolis
(Beth-Shean)
Pella
Salim
(Enon)
Dion
Gerasa
Samaria
Mt. Ebal
Ænon
Shechem
Sychar
Jacob's Well
Plain of Sharon
River Jordan
R. Jabbok
Mt. Gerizim
Antipatris
Mt. Gilead
Ramoth Gilead
MTS. OF EPHRAIM
Shiloh
Jaffa
(Joppa)
Lydda
Bethel
Rabbath Ammon
(Philadelphia)
Jabneh
(Jamnia)
Rama
Jericho
Emmaus
Bethpage
JERUSALEM
Mt. of Olives
Bethany
Azotus
Kedron
Bethlehem
Mt. Nebo
Askalon
Plain of Shephelah
MTS. OF JUDÆA
Machærus
Hebron
Gaza
R. Arnon
Wilderness of Judæa
Beer-sheba
Wady Ghuzzeh
34° 30'
35°
35° 30'
36°
32°
31°
Longitude East from Greenwich
Engraving Co., N.Y.

Chapter 25

How to Read the Gospels

The second half of the Bible is what we call the New Testament. This half stands out from the Hebrew Scripture in that it tells the story of Jesus and the development of the church in the first century AD.

The first section of the New Testament is called the Gospels.

The Gospel of Matthew
The Gospel of Mark
The Gospel of Luke
The Gospel of John

And each of these Gospels is a biography of the life of Jesus.

But what is a gospel? And why do we have four of them?

The word *gospel* in Greek is *euangelion*, meaning "good news."

A gospel was an announcement or a proclamation regarding a change of leadership within the kingdom. So in the case of the Greek Empire or the Roman Empire, when the emperor died and their successor was decided upon, a herald would go into every region, city, and town square announcing the "good news" of who their new emperor was, what their kingdom would stand for, and how the change would benefit those listening.

Caesar Augustus had a gospel message.

Alexander the Great had a gospel message.

This is how the region spoke of their emperors—with phrases and words that Jesus would later take for himself so people could comprehend what he was there to do.

Jesus entered each new city claiming that he was now King. A new kingdom had arrived. And what was the good news of Jesus' kingdom? The blind could see, the lame would walk, people with leprosy were cleansed, the deaf could hear, the dead were raised, the poor were taken care of, and the sins of humanity were forgiven.

The kingdom of God was *very* good news. In his kingdom, heaven and earth were being merged.

Now, when you read the Bible and come across the Gospels of Matthew, Mark, Luke, and John, you'll understand that each of these authors had his own perspective on his gospel announcement.

Matthew

The first gospel in the New Testament is from Matthew, one of Jesus' twelve disciples.

Matthew was a Jewish man who worked for the Roman government, but he knew the Torah (the first five books of the Old Testament) very well.

So Matthew's gospel was written with a Jewish audience in mind. He emphasized that Jesus was a new, greater version of Moses, and the true King of the Jews. Matthew focused on the teachings of Jesus more than anything else to show how Jesus was the fulfillment of Old Testament prophecy.

Mark

The second gospel is from John Mark, who actually didn't know Jesus very well (if at all), but he was close to the apostle Peter. Think of Mark's gospel as a written version of Peter's firsthand account. It's quick and to the point, written almost like a news broadcaster describing the life of Jesus to a television audience.

Mark focused on Jesus as the Son of God, the Messiah, who didn't come as a political leader but as a servant who would suffer on behalf of all humanity. Mark is the shortest of the Gospels and was written primarily to a Gentile, Roman audience.

Luke

The next gospel is from Luke, a doctor who did not know Jesus personally. He compiled his gospel based on interviews from a bunch of people who knew Jesus or were around him.

Luke was a Gentile, which is a word for someone who isn't Jewish. He was close friends with the apostle Paul, whom we'll learn a lot more about when we get to the section on the early church. Luke wrote this gospel kind of as a part one, with the book of Acts as a part two. He wrote them for a man named Theophilus (also a Gentile) as an account of the life of Jesus. As a doctor fascinated by the miracles Jesus performed, Luke focused his gospel on the humanity of Jesus.

John

Matthew, Mark, and Luke are called the Synoptic Gospels because they all shared a lot of the same stories, but the Gospel of John is over 90 percent unique compared to the others. John wrote his gospel decades later, so he had time to think through what the other gospels had missed and what was important for the early church to know about Jesus.

Known as the "Beloved Disciple," John was one of Jesus' closest friends. He focused his gospel on the claim that Jesus was God in human form, offering humanity eternal life through his sacrifice.

Each gospel was written in a unique way for a specific audience, but they all announced that the kingdom of God was at hand and would positively impact the entire world. Today, our access to these incredible messages means we can easily learn more about Jesus and the kingdom he began.

This is very good news.

One-Sentence Recap

A gospel is the proclamation of good news that a new and better kingdom—the kingdom of God—is here.

Chapter 26

The Birth and Early Life of Jesus

Matthew 1–2; Luke 1–2

At this point in time, the Israelites had been waiting centuries for the fulfillment of the promises spoken of by their prophets: that one day God would send the Messiah to establish his kingdom throughout the earth.

But they had been waiting and waiting and waiting . . .

And hope was drifting away.

Will God ever send the Savior? Or did he forget about us?

The story picks up in the hills of Jerusalem with a barren couple named Zechariah and Elizabeth. They were very old and wanted a baby, but they hadn't been able to conceive. (This might bring to mind Abraham and Sarah's barrenness too.)

Zechariah was a priest from the line of Aaron, and one day when he was working inside the temple, fulfilling his priestly duties, an archangel named Gabriel visited. The angel told Zechariah he was going to have a son named John who would prepare Israel for the Messiah, helping to usher in the messianic era they had all been waiting for.

Then the story shifts to the small town of Nazareth in the region of Galilee. Here we are introduced to Elizabeth's cousin Mary. Yes, *that* Mary.

The same angel who visited Zechariah appeared to Mary and said, "Greetings, favored woman! The Lord is with you . . . Do not be afraid, Mary, for you have found favor with God. Now listen: You will conceive and give birth to a son, and you will name him Jesus. He will be great and will be called the Son of the Most High, and the Lord God will give him the throne of his father David. He will reign over the house of Jacob forever, and his kingdom will have no end" (Luke 1:28–33).

This was the moment the Jews had been waiting for.

There was one problem: Mary, still a virgin, wasn't married. But the angel assured Mary her pregnancy would be a miraculous one, and Mary accepted this promise. But as you might imagine, her fiancé, Joseph, had a harder time accepting it.

Joseph decided to quietly call off the engagement.

But one night Joseph had a dream in which the angel confirmed Mary's story to him.

To have a child out of wedlock at that time was extremely shameful. Nobody would have believed that Mary's pregnancy was a miracle from God. The fact that Joseph agreed to remain the father of Jesus instead of leaving Mary was a miracle all its own, because now that shame was going to be placed upon him as well.

Sure enough, nine months later, Mary was nearing the end of her pregnancy. Around that time, the emperor of Rome, Caesar Augustus, sent a decree all around the world, calling the Roman citizens back to their hometowns to be registered for a census.

Joseph, a descendant of David, was from Bethlehem—so he and Mary made their way back to his hometown.

When they arrived, the city was packed. Bethlehem did not have room for everyone.

So Joseph and Mary ended up spending the night in the same place the animals were taken care of, either a stable or a shepherd's cave.

It was not an ideal spot to deliver a baby. But this was the place Jesus, the Son of God, the long-awaited Messiah, was born into.

Now while all of this was happening, a group of shepherds was nearby in the wilderness. An angel appeared to them and said, "Do not be afraid. I bring you good news that will cause great joy for all the people. Today in the town of David a Savior has been born to you; he is the Messiah, the Lord. This will be a sign to you: You will find a baby wrapped in cloths and lying in a manger" (Luke 2:10–12 NIV).

The shepherds hurried off to Bethlehem and found Mary, Joseph, and the baby just as the angel said they would. The time they had all been waiting for was finally here—and in a completely different way than they would have expected.

Meanwhile, a group of wise men (called "magi," a sort of ancient spiritual advisor) from Babylon saw a sign in the stars. The sign told them a new king had been born to lead the world into a new era. They followed the star to Jerusalem and went straight to Herod, expecting the new king to be from his bloodline—but they were shocked to discover that the child wasn't Herod's. So the wise men left Herod's palace, and the star rose again and led them straight to baby Jesus. We call these guys the "three wise men" or "three kings," but the Bible doesn't actually say how many of them there were. All we know is that they brought three generous gifts: frankincense and myrrh—two ancient perfume-like substances—and gold. These gifts would have been worth a *lot* of money in Israel.

Herod, out of fear for what might come of his throne, commanded his army to go into Bethlehem and kill every baby boy two years old or younger. Sound familiar? This parallels the story in Exodus when Moses was born.

The story was set up for the original Jewish audience to anticipate Jesus as a great leader of God's people—like Moses, but even better.

The parallels don't end there. While the Israelites fled Egypt to get away from the oppressive pharaoh, Joseph and Mary and Jesus fled Judea to escape Herod's evil plans and sought safety in Egypt.

After Herod died in 4 BC, an angel appeared to Joseph telling him they were free to return to Israel, to Nazareth, since the threat was no longer there.

So now Jesus—born in Bethlehem, raised in Nazareth—was going to grow up to become the Savior of the world, which we'll learn about in the next few chapters.

One-Sentence Recap

After centuries of Israel's waiting for the promised Messiah, Jesus was born to the virgin Mary and would grow up to become the Savior of the world.

How to Apply This Lesson to Your Life

God often works through humble and unexpected circumstances to fulfill his plan and purpose for our lives.

Chapter 27

Preparing for Ministry

Matthew 3–4; Mark 1; Luke 3–4

As Jesus' cousin John grew up, he became fully dedicated to his faith. God used him to prepare the way for the Messiah, just as the angel Gabriel had prophesied to his dad, Zechariah. All of the pieces were falling into place for Jesus' ministry to begin.

Even though the story of John is in the New Testament, he is considered the final prophet of the Old Testament before the messianic era arrived. And just as the prophets in the Old Testament were deemed odd in the eyes of society, so was John. In fact, John was extra weird.

The Bible says he was clothed in camel's hair, ate locusts and honey, and would yell out, "Repent, because the kingdom of heaven has come near!" (Matthew 3:2).

Very strange guy.

John was often found at the shore of the Jordan River baptizing everyone who needed to repent. People came from all over the region of Judea just to be baptized by John, which is how he got the nickname John the Baptist.

Earlier in the book, we talked about how the Hebrew word for "sin" means "to fail, to miss the goal, or to go astray." John was calling for repentance from sin, and the word for "repentance" is *t'shuva*, which actually means "returning." The idea behind *t'shuva* is that we are returning to who God originally created us to be—people made in his image.

So the baptism John was doing for the people was all about them publicly acknowledging how they had gone astray and wanted to renew their commitment to God. This baptism signaled that they hoped to walk in the way they were created to live.

Being baptized in the Jordan River was a way of starting over. John the Baptist wanted the people to get in line with the original plan—and he let them all know the Messiah was just around the corner.

John said to the people, "I baptize you with water for repentance, but the one who is coming after me is more powerful than I. I am not worthy to remove his sandals. He himself will baptize you with the Holy Spirit and fire" (Matthew 3:11).

One day, Jesus came down to the Jordan River from Galilee to be baptized by John too.

John was a little confused about why Jesus would want to be baptized because Jesus lived a sin-free life, but he agreed and baptized him anyway. As soon as Jesus came up out of the water, the heavens opened and the Spirit of God descended on Jesus like a dove. Then God the Father said from heaven, "This is my Son, whom I love; with him I am well pleased" (Matthew 3:17 NIV).

This was the gospel announcement, the public declaration that the kingdom of God had arrived and God was bringing the world back into order through his Son, Jesus. He was the one the people had been waiting for.

The ministry of Jesus had officially begun. It was time for him to tell the Jews that he was the fulfillment of prophecy. And where should he go to tell them? The synagogue, of course.

A synagogue was much more than a church building like we have today. A synagogue in Judaism was more of a community center. It was a place to hold worship services, hang out with friends, go to school, and even attend community meetings. The sanctuary in the middle had benches for attendees to sit during the weekly Sabbath teaching, including a special seat for the person who was reading the Torah that week. This seat was called "Moses' seat." Whoever sat in it would read from the Torah and then teach people by commenting on the text. They didn't have pastors like we do today.

One day on the Sabbath, Jesus went to the synagogue in his hometown of Nazareth and was asked to read that week's portion of Scripture. The Jewish calendar follows a specific reading plan where they read through different scriptures every week. The week Jesus was asked to read just so happened to be the most important piece of Scripture he could have read.

Jesus was handed the scroll of the prophet Isaiah. He unrolled it and read: "The Spirit of the Lord is on me, because he has anointed me to preach good news to the poor. He has sent me to proclaim release to the captives and recovery of sight to the blind, to set free the oppressed, to proclaim the year of the Lord's favor" (Luke 4:18–19).

Then Jesus rolled up the scroll, gave it back to the attendant, and sat down. With all eyes on him, waiting for whatever comments he would make on the scriptures, he began by saying, "Today as you listen, this Scripture has been fulfilled" (Luke 4:21).

He was the fulfillment of Isaiah's prophecy. The kingdom of God was being initiated around the world, and it had begun right there in a little synagogue in Nazareth. Jesus had arrived to bring good news to the poor, to bring freedom to the oppressed, to heal the sick, and to usher in a time of reset, a time of jubilee.

Everything was going to be different from now on.

One-Sentence Recap

Jesus' baptism by John the Baptist marked the beginning of his ministry, and his proclamation in the synagogue that he was the fulfillment of Isaiah's prophecy demonstrated the start of the messianic era.

How to Apply This Lesson to Your Life

If we embrace repentance and remain focused on God's plan, he will use us to bring about the kingdom of God. It won't be easy—we will go through testing—but if we remain committed, we will see God moving in miraculous ways.

Chapter 28

Calling the Disciples

Matthew 4; Mark 1; Luke 5; John 1

One thing that has gotten lost over the years is the understanding that Jesus was Jewish. His disciples, too, were Jewish. We need to understand the history of our faith from a Jewish perspective. Not only was Jesus Jewish, but he was also considered to be a great teacher or a sage. In modern times, we would call him a rabbi.

What Is a Rabbi?

A rabbi is a teacher who is an expert on the Hebrew scriptures and their interpretations. Rabbis were masters of the Torah and would have had the entire Hebrew Bible memorized, word for word, thought for thought. Can you even imagine the dedication, time, and passion needed to memorize that much Scripture? A rabbi would have done it with gusto.

They lived and breathed the holy text.

A rabbi wasn't elected or put into a position of authority through a testing process. Instead, he would have been recognized throughout the community based on his knowledge and ability to converse with other rabbis in the synagogue throughout the week. As the rabbis made names for themselves, they would create their own communities of disciples who would essentially become their mentees. You could even think of them as religious "influencers."

What Is a Disciple?

In the church today we think of discipleship more like mentorship. But in the Jewish tradition, to be a disciple of a rabbi was a major deal. Disciples didn't just want to learn what the rabbi knew; they wanted to become who the rabbi was. A disciple wanted to be a replica of the rabbi.

The rabbi would ask his students question after question, hoping to gauge their understanding of the Torah. He determined how the students would interpret certain things and whether they had memorized the Scriptures fully. The rabbi wanted to know if the students could handle being disciples.

And if the rabbi thought a kid had potential, he would say something along the lines of "Come, follow me." The kid would then leave everything behind and, for the next few years, live with the rabbi, listen to his teachings, eat with him, watch how he interacted with others, and examine his every move. The student imitated the rabbi in hopes of repeating the cycle, of one day having his own group of disciples to raise up.

Jesus as Rabbi

So as Jesus began his public ministry and spent time teaching and showcasing his interpretations of Scripture in different synagogues, the text implies he was a rabbi in his own right.

One day as Jesus was leaving the synagogue, he went to walk near the

Sea of Galilee. As he was walking, he saw two fishermen, Simon Peter and his brother Andrew, out casting their nets into the lake. This meant they had already left school to learn the family trade, likely because they weren't smart enough to keep studying under a rabbi.

Rabbi Jesus approached the two brothers: "'Come, follow me,' Jesus said, 'and I will send you out to fish for people'" (Matthew 4:19 NIV). They dropped their nets and followed Jesus, leaving everything behind, just as a kid would've done when accepted by a rabbi.

Jesus went a little farther down the shore of the lake and saw two other brothers, James the son of Zebedee and his brother John. They were out in their boat with their father, preparing their nets for a day of fishing. Jesus called out to them and asked them to follow him as well, so the brothers left their boat behind, left their father behind, left their livelihood behind, and followed Jesus.

Later on, Jesus was walking through town when he came upon a man named Philip. Jesus approached him and said, "Come, follow me." Philip ran to tell his friend Nathanael what had happened, but Nathanael was a little skeptical of who this Jesus was and why he would give Philip the opportunity to follow him. Once Nathanael met Jesus face-to-face, he, too, was given the opportunity to be a disciple.

After that, Jesus went out and saw a man named Levi (who would later be named Matthew) working in a tax collector's booth. Tax collectors were hated by the Jews because they had joined forces with the Romans to financially oppress the Jewish people. Jesus also went up to Levi and said, "Come, follow me."

To Simon Peter, Andrew, James, John, Philip, Nathanael, Matthew: "Come, follow me."

Every single one of them dropped everything they were doing and immediately left to follow Jesus.

The Bible doesn't describe the calling of the other five disciples, but you can bet they followed in the same way—each one of them dropping everything to join this rabbi, Jesus.

People from all over were following Jesus at this point. He had tons of disciples hanging on to his every word. But as his fame grew, he needed a trustworthy, close-knit group to help him bring God's kingdom to earth. So Jesus chose Simon Peter, Andrew, James, John, Philip, Bartholomew (Nathanael), Matthew (Levi), Thomas, James son of Alphaeus, Simon the Zealot, Judas son of James (also called Thaddaeus), and Judas Iscariot.

Twelve men, all between the ages of thirteen and thirty, were chosen to be his close disciples, the people he spent every waking hour alongside, his best friends.

The number twelve is also significant here because it was significant to the history of Israel. There were twelve sons of Jacob, twelve tribes of Moses, and twelve territories of David; so the number twelve was very symbolic for the original readers. Jesus was saying that through these twelve people, God was creating the future of Israel—rewriting history through this new group of twelve.

So the twelve disciples spent every minute with Jesus. They were in his vicinity 24-7, learning from him and doing everything he did in order to be just like him. Their new lives were in complete dedication to replicating Jesus.

And Jesus would soon use these twelve disciples to change the world.

One-Sentence Recap

Jesus called a group of twelve men who were told by society that they didn't have what it took to become a disciple—but Jesus looked at each of them and said, "Come, follow me," proving they had what God's kingdom needed.

How to Apply This Lesson to Your Life

Would you say Jesus is your rabbi today? Have you dedicated your life to becoming a true disciple? Not just someone who goes to church on Sunday for an hour, but someone who lives and breathes for Scripture more than anything else. This understanding of the disciple/rabbi relationship should be inspiring and sobering to us. Jesus calls us to much greater intimacy than we often realize.

Chapter 29

The Ministry of Jesus

Matthew, Mark, Luke, John

Jesus did not come to earth to start a new religion called Christianity. He came to earth to expand upon an old religion and show its followers how he was the fulfillment of all they had been waiting for.

When Jesus began his ministry, his first recorded words were, "The kingdom of God has come near. Repent and believe the good news!" (Mark 1:15 NIV). Remember what "good news" was referring to? It was the announcement that someone new was in charge and their ways were better than the old ways.

Everything Jesus did and said had to do with the kingdom of God (or kingdom of heaven, as the Gospel of Matthew says it). In modern times we don't fully understand the weight behind a new kingdom coming to the scene, but this would have meant a lot to the original audience.

When Jesus said the kingdom of God had arrived, he was saying he held the role of king. He was now ruling and reigning over a new group of people: Anyone who repented of their ways was told to separate themselves from the kingdom of the world and join the kingdom of God instead. It was a gospel message far greater than what they were currently experiencing under the Romans. To call yourself a Christian means you reside under the authority, the rule, of King Jesus, and if you are part of his kingdom, you do what he says and obey his commands. This kingdom began in Jerusalem and was being spread to the ends of the earth.

Jesus claimed that things were going to be different.

A new kingdom had arrived.

And Jesus was in charge of all of creation.

Here and now. In the present.

The Teachings of Jesus

Jesus went all throughout the region, teaching in synagogues in front of the religious elite, on the sides of hills in front of the poor and lowly, and in more private settings among his disciples.

He spent his time with people who were sick and outcast, politicians and wealthy tax collectors and sinners, inviting everyone to repent of their sin and join his kingdom. Jesus spent time around people of all walks of life in order to understand them and share the good news in ways they could individually relate to.

Matthew's gospel records a teaching of Jesus called the Sermon on the Mount (chapters 5–7). It was sort of a "remix" of the law that showed his followers what it meant to be kingdom people. It's truly a gift for us to have today. Jesus explained that his kingdom is an upside-down kingdom compared to the kinds of kingdoms they were accustomed to.

He said things like "Blessed are those who mourn, for they will be comforted" and "Blessed are the pure in heart, for they will see God" and "Blessed are the peacemakers, for they will be called sons of God" (Matthew 5:4, 8–9).

The kingdom of God wasn't taking over the old one with force and violence, but with peace and love and joy and an emphasis on holiness. This kingdom was the exact opposite of the kingdom of the world. The kingdom of God cared for the poor and sick and hurting and defenseless; it wouldn't take over in a military fashion like the powers of the world always did.

Jesus taught believers how to handle anger and lust and divorce and enemies. He taught them how to pray and fast and handle money and deal with anxiety. He went on and on, teaching about this new kingdom that had come near—God's kingdom.

Jesus basically said, "If you accept me as your Messiah, as your King, this is how you should live from here on out."

This "kingdom lifestyle" is how God planned to partner with humans to rescue and redeem the world. If people were willing to obey his teachings, the world would slowly become what God had intended it to be.

Miracles of Jesus

Not only did Jesus *teach* about the kingdom of God, but he also *showed* the people through different miracles what life was like inside the kingdom.

What is a miracle?

A miracle is when God works outside of our human, physical understanding and does something extraordinary.

Jesus used miracles to confirm his teachings and bring glory to God. The Gospels tell story after story of Jesus performing miracles for people.

Healing miracles like giving sight to the blind and curing leprosy and other illnesses.

Nature miracles like calming the storm and walking on water.

Exorcisms that cast out demons and set people free.

Provision miracles like feeding the five thousand and turning water to wine.

Each miracle Jesus performed was to show what life would be like when heaven and earth collided. In heaven there is no sickness, no possession, no chaos, and no lack—so anywhere Jesus displayed the kingdom of God, he brought wholeness, freedom, justice, peace, and provision. This is what the future would look like for all who believed.

John said in his gospel account, "Jesus did many other things as well. If every one of them were written down, I suppose that even the whole world would not have room for the books that would be written" (John 21:25 NIV).

The miracles of Jesus were numerous.

Heaven was invading earth once again.

In the early stages of Jesus' ministry, he rose in popularity just as you would imagine. He was the talk of the town, bringing the living kingdom into their present reality through his teachings and miracles. Everyone flocked to him because everyone was invited into his kingdom. When the rest of society and the religious elite cast people out from their presence, Jesus brought them closer, showing them their value and worth in God's eyes.

But this kingdom was turning out to be quite different from what the Jewish ancestors and tradition had expected it to be. And even though Jesus was doing great things, many people had hoped for someone who would take over with power and military might. They didn't want to love their enemies, as Jesus commanded. They wanted to see their enemies defeated the old-fashioned way, and it was becoming clear that Jesus wasn't interested in that kind of power. Furthermore, while they tended to focus on the external actions, Jesus focused on the heart. So the religious leaders began to speak up and question everything Jesus said.

In the church today, people will often talk negatively about the Pharisees and Sadducees and chief priests of Jesus' time, but a lot of what they believed was rooted in their fear of God. Yes, many of them missed the Messiah when he was right in front of them, and yes, they sometimes focused more on tradition than Scripture—but it's easy to see how the words and actions of Jesus would have been confusing to them. Jesus spent time hanging out with sinners, challenging the Pharisees' authority, and breaking some of the laws they had set up in addition to the law of Moses.

The tension between Jesus and the religious leaders of his day continued to escalate until Jesus declared himself the Son of God, saying he had the divine power to forgive sins.

For the Pharisees, that was the final straw. They'd had enough of Jesus and began looking for ways to kill him, which we'll explore in the next chapter.

One-Sentence Recap

The ministry of Jesus began with the announcement that the kingdom of God had arrived, and he spent the next few years talking about life in God's kingdom and showing it physically through his miracles.

How to Apply This Lesson to Your Life

When we accept Jesus as our King and Lord, he invites us to participate in the kingdom of God, bringing heaven to earth in the present, and boosting our hope for the future where he reigns for the rest of eternity.

Chapter 30

The Final Week

Matthew 21–26; Mark 11; Luke 19; John 12

The final week of Jesus' life is often referred to as the Passion Week. A lot of things happened in the days leading up to the crucifixion of Jesus, but this chapter will focus on three main events: the triumphal entry, the cleansing of the temple, and the Last Supper.

The Triumphal Entry

During Bible times, the Jews would travel to Jerusalem three times every year to celebrate three of the festivals God had commanded them to celebrate in the book of Exodus.

Scholars believe the average population of Jerusalem was between twenty thousand and thirty thousand at any time, but during the festivals, it would grow to hundreds of thousands. The historian Josephus even recounted one year that the population grew to 2.7 million![1]

The final week of Jesus' life took place at the beginning of Passover week, when the city was roaring with life. People came from all over the region to sacrifice at the temple and celebrate God's faithfulness as a community. This year was most likely even more exciting, as word had spread around Judea about this man named Jesus and the wondrous miracles he was performing. The anticipation had built for his arrival.

As Jesus and the disciples neared Jerusalem, they stopped on the Mount of Olives. There he sent two disciples with specific instructions: "Go into the village ahead of you. At once you will find a donkey tied there with her colt. Untie them and bring them to me" (Matthew 21:2–3).

Kind of strange, right? That's because context is key.

According to Old Testament prophecy, Zechariah had said, "Rejoice greatly, Daughter Zion! Shout in triumph, Daughter Jerusalem! Look, your King is coming to you; he is righteous and victorious, humble and riding on a donkey, on a colt, the foal of a donkey" (Zechariah 9:9). This was all a fulfillment of prophecy. Jesus had to ride in on a donkey, even though he could have walked. The Mount of Olives was literally across a field from the entrance of Jerusalem, so it wouldn't have taken much time at all—but this style of arrival was necessary to fulfill the Scriptures.

As Jesus entered Jerusalem, a large crowd gathered on the road to welcome their new king. They placed their cloaks and palm branches on the road, shouting: "Hosanna to the Son of David! Blessed is he who comes in the name of the Lord! Hosanna in the highest heaven!" (Matthew 21:9).

There's so much here to understand.

Jesus was riding a donkey, not riding a horse like a conquering king.

By riding in, he was displaying himself as the "King of the Jews."

Palm branches represented victory and kingship at that time.

The word *hosanna* means "save us."

The crowd thought *this* was the moment; they expected Jesus to arrive as their political king, ready to overthrow the Roman government, just as the prophecies of old suggested. He was going to conquer and usher in the messianic era, and everything was going to be different from here on out.

But things took a turn when they woke up the next morning. Jesus didn't go to the Roman authorities but went straight for the outer courts of the temple instead.

The Cleansing of the Temple

As Jesus entered the temple courts, he saw all of the money changers and merchants selling animals for sacrifices to the visiting travelers. The place was chaotic. It seemed as if the people cared more about taxes and the business behind the temple sacrifices than they did about it being a house of worship.

The temple was supposed to be a place for God and man to connect, not a place for profit-making.

So Jesus, out of holy anger, went throughout the courts and began driving out all those who were buying and selling. He went to the tables of the money changers and the benches of those selling doves and flipped them over as well. He said, "It is written, my house will be called a house of prayer, but you are making it a den of thieves!" (Matthew 21:13).

At this moment, more and more people must have realized that Jesus wasn't coming to take over politically, but spiritually. He was zealous for worship to return to its pure form. Fewer distractions and more connection with God.

The Last Supper

A few days later, a pivotal event of Passion Week took place: the Passover meal, which we now call "the Last Supper" in the church.

The Passover meal was and is a time for the Jews to look back on the story of the exodus and remember everything God did for them.[2]

Remember, on the last night of the Israelites' enslavement, before Moses led them out of Egypt, God performed one final miraculous act: the killing of the firstborn from each Egyptian family. The Israelites were told to slaughter a spotless, unblemished lamb and wipe its blood over the doorposts of their homes. Then, when the Lord went from home to home that night, he "passed over" any home that was covered by the clean blood. The blood marking had protected God's people.

The Israelites did as God commanded, waiting up all night to make sure their firstborn would survive and that God would be faithful to his word.

The next morning, everyone who had covered their doorpost in the blood of the lamb was safe. Soon after, God led the Israelites through the Red Sea and eventually into their promised land.

God commanded the Israelites to celebrate a meal every year in remembrance of this story—to look back at God's faithfulness to his people and dwell on how the Jewish nation had been reborn. But Passover was also celebrated with a hope for the future. They knew God would one day set them free from "exile" again and lead them into a new promised land, God's kingdom, under his messianic King. God would establish a new covenant with his people, and all of their sins would be forgiven.

So what did a Passover meal look like?

During a Passover meal the family would walk through the entire storyline of the exodus, eating and drinking certain things at certain times to symbolically relive the escape from Egypt. This meal that we read about in the Gospels, this Last Supper, was full of symbolism for what was about to happen to (and through) Jesus.

The Passover meal was mainly based on Exodus 6:6–8, where God said,

> "I am the LORD, and I will bring you out from under the yoke of the Egyptians. I will free you from being slaves to them, and I will redeem you with an outstretched arm and with mighty acts of judgment. I will take you as my own people, and I will be your God. Then you will know that I am the LORD your God, who brought you out from under the yoke of the Egyptians. And I will bring you to the land I swore with uplifted hand to give to Abraham, to Isaac and to Jacob. I will give it to you as a possession. I am the LORD." (NIV)

Notice how these verses are broken into four promises:

1. I will bring you out from under the yoke of the Egyptians.
2. I will free you from enslavement.
3. I will redeem you with an outstretched arm.
4. I will take you as my people, and I will be your God.

Each promise was represented by a glass of wine throughout the meal.

To begin, after lighting the Passover candles, each attendee would take their first cup of wine, known as the Cup of Sanctification. The word *sanctification* is just a big word meaning "to be made holy or set apart." Drinking this first cup represented God bringing the Israelites out from under the yoke of the Egyptians and setting them apart. Celebrants would say a series of blessings and thank God for all he had done for them.

The host would then lead the people through a series of actions representing different parts of the exodus story—such as washing their hands, dipping herbs into salt water, and breaking matzo bread into three pieces.

The second cup of wine, the Cup of Deliverance, was consumed right afterward to commemorate God freeing them from slavery as well as the bondage of sin. They would thank God for freedom from both Pharaoh and the Evil One.

Dinner was next, consisting of the lamb God commanded them to sacrifice. During the meal of Jesus and his disciples, Jesus stood up and took the matzo bread, which symbolized a sin-free life, and broke the bread, saying, "Take and eat it; this is my body" (Matthew 26:26). This is the first part of Communion (also called the Eucharist or the Lord's Supper) for us in the church. We break bread to remember that Jesus' body was broken for us on the cross, and that through his sacrifice, our sins have been covered.

After eating of the matzo and finishing their meal, they would have poured themselves the third cup, the Cup of Redemption, representing how God would redeem them. The Bible says that after Jesus gave thanks for this cup, he said, "This is my blood of the covenant, which is poured out for many for the forgiveness of sins" (Matthew 26:28).

He was going to die for his people.

The time was almost upon them—when God would rescue his people from the stronghold of sin, and they would be in a new covenant with God. This was much bigger than being freed from the Romans; this was a new way of living, a way the powers of evil couldn't stop.

The fourth cup of wine was then poured for the disciples, the Cup of Restoration, which was a prophetic cup of wine. It looked forward to the day when God would be with his people again in the new kingdom. They would then praise God and sing and dance for the future restoration to come. It was a party, after all!

Even though the Passover seder was over, this meal was only the beginning for Jesus. In the next chapter, we will learn all about what happened next with Jesus' trial, crucifixion, and ultimate resurrection.

One-Sentence Recap

The final week of Jesus' life was marked by many events that reveal his identity as the messianic King and how he would establish the new covenant through his sacrificial death.

How to Apply This Lesson to Your Life

As Christians we need to recognize Jesus as our true King and spend time remembering what he did for us, with an expectant hope for all he will do in the future.

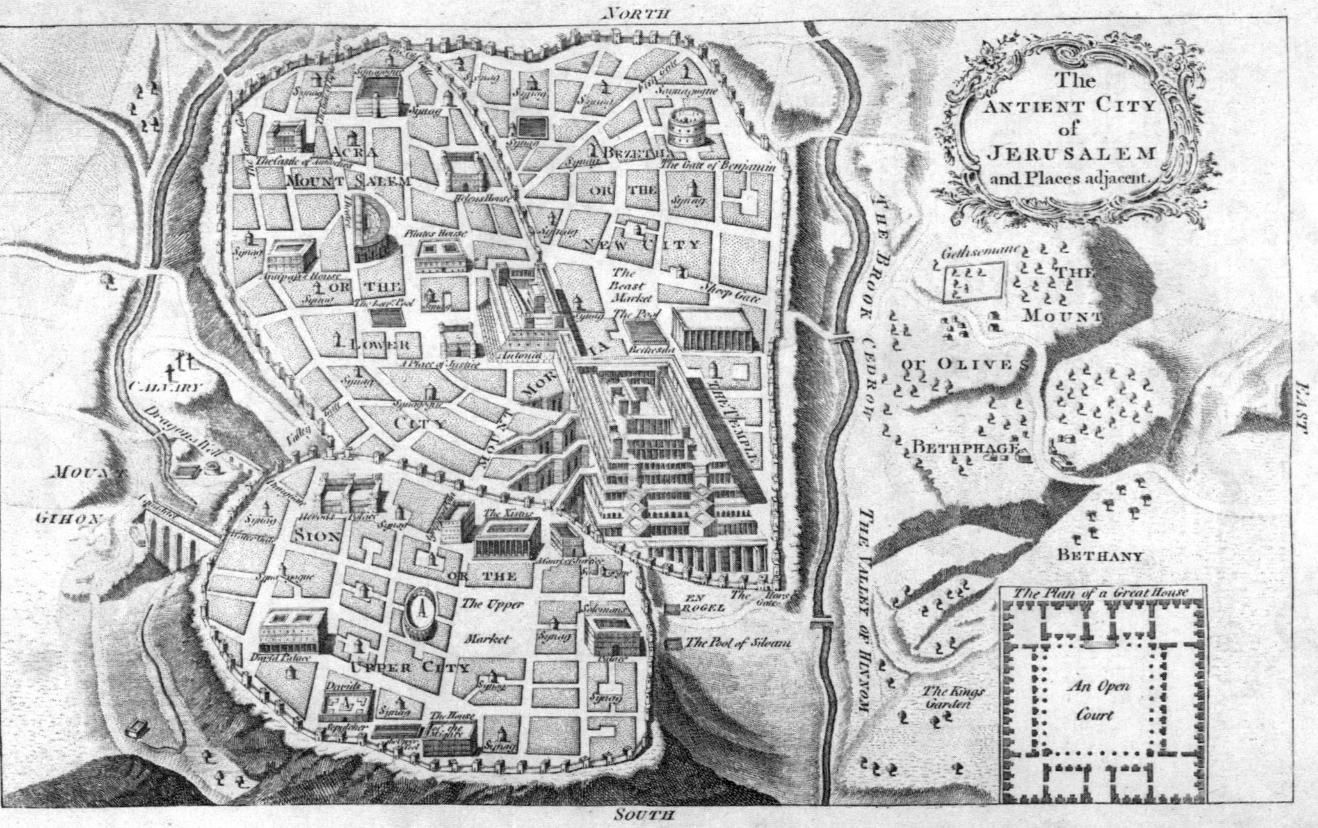

The ANTIENT CITY of JERUSALEM and Places adjacent.
NORTH
SOUTH
EAST
WEST
ACRA
MOUNT SALEM
The Castle of Antonia
Pilates House
LOWER
OR THE
CITY
A Place of Justice
Antonia
MORIA
BEZETHA
The Gate of Benjamin
OR THE
NEW CITY
The Beast Market
The Pool
Bethesda
Sheep Gate
Synagogue
THE TEMPLE
SION
OR THE
The Upper Market
UPPER CITY
David Palace
Davids
The House of the Mighty
Sepulcher
The Xistus
EN ROGEL
The Horse Gate
The Pool of Siloam
CALVARY
Dragons Well
MOUNT
GIHON
THE BROOK CEDROW
THE VALLEY OF HINNOM
Gethsemane
THE MOUNT OF OLIVES
BETHPHAGE
BETHANY
The Kings Garden
The Plan of a Great House
An Open Court

Chapter 31

Trial and Crucifixion

Matthew 26–27; Mark 14–15; Luke 22–23; John 18–19

After the Last Supper meal, Jesus and his disciples went back to Gethsemane where they were staying, about a half-mile walk through the Kidron Valley once leaving the gates of Jerusalem.

William Barclay said this about the Kidron Valley at this time of year:

> All the Passover lambs were killed in the Temple, and the blood of the lambs was poured on the altar as an offering to God. The number of lambs slain for the Passover was immense. On one occasion, thirty years later than the time of Jesus, a census was taken and the number was 256,000. We may imagine what the Temple courts were like when the blood of all these lambs was dashed on to the altar. From the altar there was a channel down to the brook Kedron, and through that channel the blood of the Passover lambs drained away. When Jesus crossed the brook Kedron it would still be red with the blood of the lambs which had been sacrificed; and as he did so, the thought of his own sacrifice would surely be vivid in his mind.[1]

Jesus chose the timing of his crucifixion to illustrate what was about to happen to him. He was the Passover Lamb that was soon to be led to the slaughter.

Once they arrived in Gethsemane, Jesus took a few of the disciples with him out to the garden to pray. Jesus prayed with great intensity, as it seems he was reflecting on what was about to happen. The weight of the world's sin was about to be placed on his shoulders.

As Jesus was speaking to his disciples, the chief priests, the elders, and a large crowd arrived to arrest him. His disciple Judas Iscariot led the way, having betrayed Jesus for a paltry thirty pieces of silver. Judas had told the crowd that the man he greeted with a kiss would be Jesus. So Judas went up to Jesus and said, "Greetings, Rabbi!" and kissed him. Jesus responded, "Do what you came for, friend."

And immediately the chief priests, elders, and temple police arrested Jesus.

Jesus' Trial

Jesus was brought to the high priest Caiaphas and the rest of the religious leaders, who now had to figure out how they could charge Jesus. The truth was, while Jesus had been a huge thorn in their side, he hadn't actually committed any crimes. They needed to come up with a lie to justify executing him. And they couldn't execute someone without the approval of Pontius Pilate, the Roman governor of Judea.

Early the next morning, the chief priests and elders handed Jesus over to Pilate, claiming he was dangerous and needed to be executed. Pilate, who was known as the king of the Jews, asked Jesus, "Are *you* the king of the Jews?"

"You have said so," Jesus replied.

Even though Jesus wasn't guilty of the claims the religious leaders were placing on him, he remained silent and didn't defend himself against any of the trumped-up charges. Pilate tried to cut a deal with the leaders by letting another prisoner go free in hopes of reducing Jesus' sentence to jail time.

But the people kept yelling, "Crucify him! Crucify him!"

When Pilate asked why, they just responded with: "Crucify him! Crucify him!"

Pilate washed his hands in front of the people to demonstrate that he wouldn't be held responsible for Jesus' innocent bloodshed—then he handed Jesus over to the people to be crucified.

The Crucifixion

The governor's soldiers took Jesus into the Praetorium and gathered all the soldiers around him. They stripped him naked, placed a purple robe on him, twisted a crown of thorns and pushed it into his skull, and placed a staff in his right hand (all to represent royalty—their way of taunting him and his claims). The soldiers knelt before Jesus and mocked him, saying, "Hail, king of the Jews!" (Mark 15:18; John 19:3).

They spit on him.

They beat him.

And when Jesus was dripping in blood, barely able to stand, they paraded him through the streets of Jerusalem toward his crucifixion. He *was* the true King of the Jews, but he was being made a mockery in front of everyone.

They arrived at the place of crucifixion, Golgotha, which means "the place of the skull." It was a place where everyone in the city could see what would happen to them if they chose to do what Jesus did.

Theologians N. T. Wright and Michael F. Bird wrote, "Crucifixion was a brutal and barbaric form of execution . . . Naked half-dead men dying a protracted death for days on end, covered in blood and flies, their flesh gnawed at by rats, their members ripped at by wild dogs, their faces pecked by crows, the victims mocked and jeered by sadistic torturers and other bystanders, while relatives nearby, weeping uncontrollably, would be helpless to do anything for them."[2]

Crucifixion was the most humiliating possible way to die.

The guards drove nails into Jesus' hands and feet and erected the cross for all to see. They placed a sign above his head that read, "This Is the King of the Jews."

And the Bible says that at three in the afternoon, Jesus called out with a loud voice: "Father, into your hands I commit my spirit," and he breathed his last breath (Luke 23:46 NIV).

At that exact moment, inside the temple, the large curtain separating the holy of holies from the rest of the temple was torn from top to bottom. The one place where God's presence was meant to be, his home on earth, was no longer contained to one location.

The whole world was about to be his temple. A new day had arrived.

Jesus' Burial

The Jewish people celebrated seven major feasts every year as commanded of them in the book of Exodus—four in the spring and three in the fall.

Three of the spring feasts took place during an eight-day period beginning with Passover, followed by the Feast of Unleavened Bread for the next seven days, and in the middle of that, on the day after the first Sabbath during Passover week, they celebrated the Feast of Firstfruits.

Passover was about remembering the exodus from Egypt and the end of exile.

The Feast of Unleavened Bread was about remembering the sacrifice necessary to remove one's sin.

The Feast of Firstfruits was about thanking God for a new beginning, a new harvest season.

Three celebrations crammed into eight days.

Another thing to consider is that in Judaism, the day begins at sundown because the Jewish people went by a lunar calendar instead of a solar calendar. So after Jesus died in the afternoon—just as the sun was beginning to set and just before the Feast of Unleavened Bread was about to begin—one of Jesus' wealthy disciples went to Pilate and asked if he could bury Jesus' body. Pilate agreed, and Joseph took the body, wrapped it in a clean linen cloth, and placed it in his own personal garden tomb. Then a stone was rolled in front of the tomb, and Jesus was left while the rest of the city began its next celebration.

Out of fear that Jesus' followers would steal the body and claim he had risen from the dead, Pilate had the tomb secured as best as he could. He even set guards in front of it so Jesus' followers couldn't try any funny business.

Can you imagine what it must have been like for all the early followers of Jesus who had put their trust and faith in him as their Messiah—but then all of a sudden, he was dead?

The story was at its climax, and then it just ended. Silence. Flatline.

How confusing that must have been!

Why Did Jesus Have to Die?

Have you ever asked this question before? Like, every Christian knows Jesus died for our sins, but what does that really mean? Why did he have to die?

Well, going back to the beginning of the Bible, we learned that sin and evil separated humans from a relationship with God. God is holy, so he can't be near anything sinful. This is a problem for a being who wants to be in relationship with his creation. We are full of sin, so a barrier exists between us and God. The apostle Paul wrote in a letter to the Romans that "all have sinned and fall short of the glory of God" (Romans 3:23).

So what did God do to help restore that relationship? He first put a justice system in place consisting of animal sacrifices. When the Israelites sacrificed unblemished animals, the blood would temporarily cover their sin. This system was built on the concept of substituting the death of one thing for the life of another.

But these sacrifices didn't cover sin forever. The Israelites were in a never-ending cycle of sin and sacrifice, and it wasn't realistic long-term.

A sinless *human* willing to be sacrificed, on the other hand, would cover the sins of humanity once and for all. So God sent his Son, sinless and spotless, as the perfect and final sacrifice to end the sacrificial system and usher in a new age for humanity, a new level in possible relationship with God.

Paul also said in Romans, "The wages of sin is death, but the gift of God is eternal life in Christ Jesus our Lord" (6:23). The death of Jesus on the cross was God's ultimate demonstration of love for us. He was the substitute for our sins, meaning he took our punishment (death) and gave us the gift of life instead. If Jesus hadn't died in this way, there would be no forgiveness of sins. Now when God looks at us, he sees the redemptive work of his Son and loves us even though we still sin.

Our relationship with God has been restored, creating a new covenant between God and humanity. We now have eternal life through faith in Jesus.

In the next chapter we'll see how the cross will become the ultimate symbol of God's victory over evil.

One-Sentence Recap

Jesus was crucified as an innocent man to atone for the sins of humanity.

How to Apply This Lesson to Your Life

By placing our faith in Jesus and accepting his sacrifice as our own, we can be set free from the grip of sin and live under the new covenant with God for the rest of eternity.

Chapter 32

Resurrection and Ascension

Matthew 28; Mark 16; Luke 24; John 20–21

After Jesus died, on the following Sunday, the city began celebrating the Feast of Firstfruits. On this day, the Jews would bring the first portion of their harvest to the temple in Jerusalem as an offering, to thank God for the harvest season and ask him to provide a fruitful harvest to come.

On the morning of the Feast of Firstfruits, when everyone else would have been going to the temple with their share of crops, Mary Magdalene and the other Mary went to the tomb of Jesus in hopes of preparing his body for final burial. They weren't really sure how they would get in, since the stone had been in place for days. But all of a sudden there was a violent earthquake, and an angel of the Lord appeared. He rolled back the stone from the tomb and sat on top of it.

Everyone froze. The Bible says the guards "became like dead men" (Matthew 28:4).

The angel said to the women, "Don't be afraid, because I know you are looking for Jesus who was crucified. He is not here. For he has risen, just as he said. Come and see the place where he lay. Then go quickly and tell his disciples, 'He has risen from the dead and indeed he is going ahead of you to Galilee; you will see him there.' Listen, I have told you" (Matthew 28:5–7).

Jesus rose from the dead during the Feast of Firstfruits. He was the initial offering, paving the way for the rest of us to one day rise from the dead as well.

Everything would be different now.

Resurrection would be the new way of life.

Eternity wasn't something to come; eternal life began at that moment.

Jesus was showing that a new covenant was in place between God and humankind, and the kingdom of God now reigned supreme. Even though evil was and is present all over the world, we can have hope for the future *because* Jesus rose from the dead.

Everything he said while he was alive the first time had come true. As Christians, our entire faith is based on whether we believe Jesus rose from the dead. If we don't believe in his resurrection, Jesus was just a great teacher and miracle worker.

But since he did rise from the dead, we believe he was God incarnate. He defeated death, hell, and the grave.

We need to believe with everything inside of us that the tomb is empty and Jesus is risen. Do we really believe the Easter story? If we do, it changes everything. The world is now a new creation, a new beginning, having started over in the way God originally intended with Eden—and, as we'll see in the next few chapters, he intends to partner with us to create it, with Jesus as our example.

The resurrection of Christ was the beginning of God's kingdom, heaven on earth.

After rising from the dead, Jesus spent the next forty days appearing to the disciples and his followers. He even appeared to a group of over five hundred people at one time, demonstrating that the resurrection had taken place and commissioning them out into the world.

Even Jesus was different at this point. The text makes it sound like he was physically unrecognizable because he was in his redeemed, resurrected body. We don't know what that might have looked like, but we know our resurrected bodies will be flawless, free from the damage of sin.

Mary Magdalene didn't even recognize Jesus at first. Neither did two of his other followers as they walked toward a town called Emmaus. Jesus came up to them and walked alongside them, but they couldn't tell it was him. Jesus asked what they were talking about because they seemed sad and discouraged. They replied,

> "Are you the only one visiting Jerusalem who does not know the things that have happened there in these days?"
> "What things?" [Jesus] asked.
> "About Jesus of Nazareth," they replied. "He was a prophet, powerful in word and deed before God and all the people. The chief priests and our rulers handed him over to be sentenced to death, and they crucified him; but we had hoped that he was the one who was going to redeem Israel. And what is more, it is the third day since all this took place. In addition, some of our women amazed us. They went to the tomb early this morning but didn't find his body. They came and told us that they had seen a vision of angels, who said he was alive. Then some of our companions went to the tomb and found it just as the women had said, but they did not see Jesus." (Luke 24:18–24 NIV)

Jesus, still in disguise, told these travelers how foolish they were for not realizing that the Messiah needed to suffer in order to usher in the messianic era. He went on to explain the scriptures to them. When they reached Emmaus, the two disciples invited Jesus to stay with them. They had dinner together, and the moment Jesus took the bread and gave thanks to God for it, the eyes of the men were opened; they recognized Jesus for who he truly was.

But then he disappeared. Poof. Gone. Vanished.

Things were different now.

That same evening, the disciples were together in a house. The Gospel of John says the doors were locked because they were afraid of the Jewish leaders coming after them regarding Jesus' missing body. Suddenly, Jesus showed up out of nowhere. He literally just stood next to them in the house and said, "Peace be with you!" Then he showed them his hands with the holes from the nails that had pierced them.

Jesus could walk through walls.
But he was also in human form and could be touched.

Things. Were. Different. Now.

Jesus had the disciples meet him on the mountain near the Sea of Galilee, the same place where he first called them to follow him. It was where everything began for the disciples, where their lives were changed forever. And at this place, Jesus commissioned them, saying, "All authority has been given to me in heaven and on earth. Go, therefore, and make disciples of all nations, baptizing them in the name of the Father and of the Son and of the Holy Spirit, teaching them to observe everything I have commanded you. And remember, I am with you always, to the end of the age" (Matthew 28:18–20).

The responsibility to expand the kingdom of God was now in their hands. Just as Jesus made them disciples, he was now calling them to do the same for others: to teach people, to heal people, to cast out demons, to baptize them, to show the world what it meant to live a kingdom lifestyle. In the church, we call this the "Great Commission," and as followers of Jesus, this commission is also our responsibility.

So how would Jesus' message spread on earth? Through us! God chose to partner with us to spread the kingdom, to bring the rest of the world under his authority and rule. Everywhere the kingdom reaches, Jesus becomes Lord and King of that area. In your school, your home, your city, your job—wherever the kingdom touches—Jesus becomes Lord and King.

It's up to us now.

After spending more time with the disciples, Jesus brought them back to the Mount of Olives, just outside of Jerusalem, and said to them, "Do not leave Jerusalem, but wait for the gift my Father promised, which you have heard me speak about. For John baptized with water, but in a few days you will be baptized with the Holy Spirit" (Acts 1:4–5 NIV).

The disciples still didn't understand what was happening. They still thought he was going to rise to power and restore Israel now that he was back in human form. But Jesus said to them, "It is not for you to know times or periods that the Father has set by his own authority. But you will receive power when the Holy Spirit has come on you, and you will be my witnesses in Jerusalem, in all Judea and Samaria, and to the ends of the earth" (Acts 1:7–8).

As Jesus was in the middle of speaking, he was taken up to heaven.

The disciples, shocked at what they just witnessed, continued to stare blankly at the sky, wondering what was next. Then suddenly, once again out of nowhere, two angels showed up and said, "Men of Galilee, why do you stand looking up into heaven? This same Jesus, who has been taken from you into heaven, will come in the same way that you have seen him going into heaven" (Acts 1:11).

Jesus left, but he is coming back. We don't know when, but we know how: in the same way they saw him going into heaven.

Jesus is now on the throne in heaven, running the show as King and as Lord. Authority is his. That doesn't mean bad things don't happen anymore. But it means the plan has been initiated. Eternity began with his resurrection, and now we are commissioned to spend our lives spreading the kingdom of God until he returns.

But the disciples had to wait in Jerusalem until the promised Holy Spirit arrived—an event we'll learn more about in the next chapter.

One-Sentence Recap

Jesus' resurrection, appearances to the disciples, commissioning, and ascension to heaven showed his victory over death and placement on the throne in heaven as King and Lord of all.

How to Apply This Lesson to Your Life

We have the same commission the disciples were given: to spread the kingdom of God all throughout the world.

Part Eight

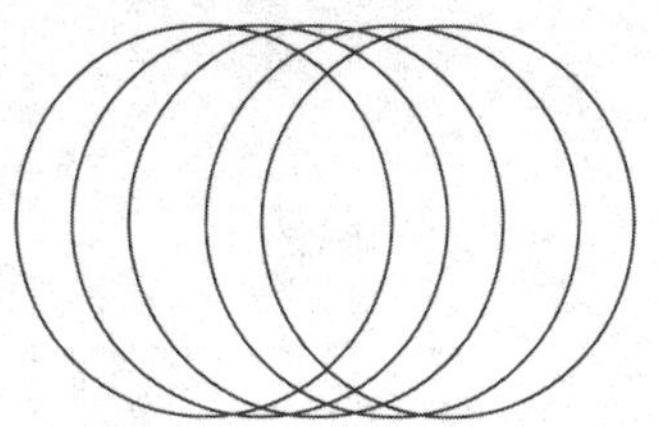

THE EARLY CHURCH

Chapter 33

Pentecost and the Holy Spirit

Acts 1–2

After Jesus' ascension, the disciples returned to Jerusalem, full of joy and expectancy for what God was going to do next.

Ten days later, Jerusalem was packed again because it was time to celebrate Pentecost. Pentecost takes place seven weeks after Passover and is another celebration of the harvest. Pentecost back then was more focused on the late harvest season, which consisted of wheat and higher-quality grains compared to the early harvest celebration.

Thousands of Jewish people were in town from all over the ancient world, bringing their offering to the temple and celebrating all God would provide for them during that harvest season.

On the morning of Pentecost, a large group of the disciples were together for their morning prayer, when a violent wind came into the house where they were sitting. Fire followed behind the wind, and what looked like tongues of fire came and rested on each of the disciples.

The Holy Spirit had arrived.

But what was going on? What was with the wind and fire?

The original readers would have understood this as a divine sign. The theme of wind and fire was repeated all throughout the Old Testament as signs of God's presence.

Remember when Moses met with God on top of Mount Sinai? God came down to the mountain in a big, windy storm and fire. From there, he made a covenant with the people of Israel and gave Moses the Ten Commandments.

Remember when the Israelites built the tabernacle for God to dwell with them in the wilderness? God's presence filled the tabernacle with a mighty rushing wind. God even led the Israelites through the wilderness with a cloud during the day and a pillar of fire at night, so they always knew he was with them.

Remember when Solomon built the temple? God's presence filled the temple's holy of holies with a cloud. Then when Solomon dedicated the temple with a sacrifice, fire came down from heaven and consumed the sacrifices.

Wind and fire.

Throughout the Old Testament the presence of God had been contained to one location: the temple. The temple was where heaven and earth collided. It was the center of the world, the holiest place on earth.

But things were going to be different now.

Now when the wind and fire came blazing into the house where the disciples were praying, they would have understood that the temple was no longer a building. It was a community of people. The temple was now inside every follower of Jesus. The overlap of heaven and earth was no longer just in Jerusalem, but everywhere the Christians were.

This changed everything.

From the beginning, God has wanted to live among his people. We saw this in the garden of Eden, the tabernacle, and the temple, but sin was always in the way. No person covered in sin could come into contact with God's holiness.

But Jesus made a way.

As John puts it in his gospel, "The Word became flesh and dwelt among us. We observed his glory, the glory as the one and only Son from the Father, full of grace and truth" (John 1:14).

As followers of Jesus, we believe in the redemptive work he performed on the cross, which covered all our sins. God can now dwell among his people, inside his people, through the Holy Spirit.

We are the new temple.

So as these tongues of fire rested upon the disciples and they were filled with the Holy Spirit, they began to speak in other languages they hadn't known before. Remember, people from all over the world were in Jerusalem for Pentecost, so the disciples went outside and began talking to them all in their own native languages, sharing the gospel of Jesus. The people were amazed and confused, and some even accused them of drunkenness because the languages sounded like gibberish in their ears.

Peter got up to address the crowd with an epic first sermon, to explain what was taking place before their eyes. He said:

> "Fellow Jews and all of you who live in Jerusalem, let me explain this to you; listen carefully to what I say. These people are not drunk, as you

suppose. It's only nine in the morning! No, this is what was spoken by the prophet Joel:

"'In the last days, God says,
I will pour out my Spirit on all people.
Your sons and daughters will prophesy,
your young men will see visions,
your old men will dream dreams.
Even on my servants, both men and women,
I will pour out my Spirit in those days,
and they will prophesy.
I will show wonders in the heavens above
and signs on the earth below,
blood and fire and billows of smoke.
The sun will be turned to darkness
and the moon to blood
before the coming of the great and glorious day of the Lord.
And everyone who calls
on the name of the Lord will be saved.'

"Fellow Israelites, listen to this: Jesus of Nazareth was a man accredited by God to you by miracles, wonders and signs, which God did among you through him, as you yourselves know. This man was handed over to you by God's deliberate plan and foreknowledge; and you, with the help of wicked men, put him to death by nailing him to the cross. But God raised him from the dead, freeing him from the agony of death, because it was impossible for death to keep its hold on him. David said about him:

"'I saw the Lord always before me.
Because he is at my right hand,
I will not be shaken.
Therefore my heart is glad and my tongue rejoices;
my body also will rest in hope,
because you will not abandon me to the realm of the dead,
you will not let your holy one see decay.

> You have made known to me the paths of life;
> you will fill me with joy in your presence.'
>
> "Fellow Israelites, I can tell you confidently that the patriarch David died and was buried, and his tomb is here to this day. But he was a prophet and knew that God had promised him on oath that he would place one of his descendants on his throne. Seeing what was to come, he spoke of the resurrection of the Messiah, that he was not abandoned to the realm of the dead, nor did his body see decay. God has raised this Jesus to life, and we are all witnesses of it. Exalted to the right hand of God, he has received from the Father the promised Holy Spirit and has poured out what you now see and hear. For David did not ascend to heaven, and yet he said,
>
> "'The Lord said to my Lord:
> "Sit at my right hand
> until I make your enemies
> a footstool for your feet."'
>
> "Therefore let all Israel be assured of this: God has made this Jesus, whom you crucified, both Lord and Messiah." (Acts 2:14–36 NIV)

When the people before him asked what they ought to do in response to this message, Peter told them: "Repent and be baptized, every one of you, in the name of Jesus Christ for the forgiveness of your sins. And you will receive the gift of the Holy Spirit. The promise is for you and your children and for all who are far off—for all whom the Lord our God will call" (Acts 2:38–39 NIV). Peter wasn't telling them to convert to a new religion like we may expect a preacher to do today. No, his audience was Jewish, and he was showing them how Jesus was the next step in their faith. Jesus was the long-awaited Messiah their ancestors had spoken of long ago. For the first decade after the ascension, the entire church (though it wasn't even called "church" yet) was made up of Jewish people who believed their Messiah had arrived.

The Bible says three thousand people were added to the followers of Jesus on Pentecost, and then many, many more in the following days.

This is a story of redemption.

The kingdom of God is here.

And just as Jesus taught his disciples to pray, "Your will be done on earth as it is in heaven" (Matthew 6:10), we have the responsibility to merge heaven and earth. It's no longer about our wills and desires and choices about right and wrong. No, to live in the kingdom of God means going back to God's original plan, learning how to be obedient to him, fearing him, and spreading his love, justice, and mercy all throughout the earth. To take the world back from the Enemy and bring light to the darkness. Bringing God's kingdom to the kingdoms of the world.

Every person who receives the Holy Spirit is the new temple of God. The goal is to make the whole world his temple. It began with the disciples in the house on Pentecost, and it continues with us today. One day, Jesus will complete his work. But as long as we are here on earth, we have a job to do.

So as these new converts left Jerusalem and brought the gospel of Jesus back to their cities, the kingdom began to spread. Jesus was now King of the world. And these followers were living like it.

This story is the birth of the church. Followers of Jesus were tasked with the responsibility to spread the gospel message around the world, and that's exactly what we see them doing, empowered by the Holy Spirit.

One-Sentence Recap

The Holy Spirit arrived with great power on the day of Pentecost, and Peter delivered a powerful message to everyone in Jerusalem, making this day the launch of the church.

How to Apply This Lesson to Your Life

As followers of Jesus who received the Holy Spirit, we are now mini temples all over the world—and as we follow God's will for our lives each day, we expand the kingdom of God here on earth.

Chapter 34

Spreading the Gospel

Acts

Just before Jesus ascended to heaven, he told the disciples, "You will receive power when the Holy Spirit has come on you, and you will be my witnesses in Jerusalem, in all Judea and Samaria, and to the ends of the earth" (Acts 1:8).

So when the Holy Spirit arrived, they were empowered to take the gospel message from Jerusalem, the hub of the Jewish faith, and spread it among the Gentiles throughout the known world. Luke wrote the book of Acts, which tells the story of the early church's growth from AD 30 to 60—beginning in Jerusalem, spreading to Judea and Samaria, and then to the rest of the world.

The Church in Jerusalem

The disciples began by preaching and sharing the good news all around Jerusalem. The Bible says they were in the temple courts every single day, telling the Jews about the life, death, and resurrection of Jesus.

The religious leaders who had favored Jesus' crucifixion now had a real problem with the disciples. They were claiming there was another way to get to God. They were claiming the Jews didn't have to go to the temple anymore or make sacrifices. People could receive the Holy Spirit personally and have nonstop, direct access to God the Father through the work of Jesus.

That was a major issue for the religious leaders of the time because the claims were considered blasphemous. Blasphemy was a big deal in ancient Israel. It was such a big deal that one of the preachers of the early Jerusalem church was stoned to death. The preacher's name was Stephen—a man whom we remember as the first Christian martyr—and his execution began a wave of severe persecution around Jerusalem, scattering fleeing believers out into Judea and Samaria.

To Judea and Samaria

The scattering into Judea and Samaria ended up being a blessing for the early church. Now the gospel message could travel farther outside the city.

Two important things happened during this time frame: Saul had an encounter with Jesus. And Peter had a dream.

A man named Saul was a very involved, active Jewish leader from the city of Tarsus. He was also a Pharisee. Not only was he a Pharisee, but he had also been educated under the great rabbi Gamaliel. Saul was kind of like an Ivy League Pharisee, with an expertise in Jewish thought that would have been respected almost everywhere he went. Saul hated followers of Jesus because he thought they were blaspheming the law and going against their faith. So he dedicated his life to stamping out this new belief.

During the stoning of Stephen, Saul was right there, cheering them on, filled with rage. He would go from house to house, dragging the new followers of Jesus out into the streets to persecute them. He even got a letter from the high priest allowing him to go to the great city of Damascus to bring any followers back to Jerusalem as prisoners.

Saul's goal was to stop the gospel message from going any further.

While Saul was on his way to Damascus, a light from heaven flashed around him and he heard a voice say,

> "Saul, Saul, why are you persecuting me?"
> "Who are you, Lord?" Saul said.
> "I am Jesus, the one you are persecuting," he replied. "But get up and go into the city, and you will be told what you must do." (Acts 9:4–6)

Saul had been persecuting Jesus' followers because he didn't believe they were telling the truth—but now he was encountering the risen Jesus himself. Sometimes God has to stop us in our tracks to get his point across, and this is exactly what happened here with Saul. God can use anyone for his plans—even someone who wanted to kill his followers.

Saul ended up getting baptized, and he began preaching the gospel. All throughout Damascus, he proclaimed that Jesus was the true Son of God, the Messiah they had been waiting for. Everyone who heard him was astonished because they knew he had originally been heading to Damascus to arrest believers. Now here he was, preaching their same message. As we'll soon see, Saul was to become one of the most important figures in the early church. In fact, he was about to become one of the most important religious figures of all time.

While all of this was happening with Saul, Peter continued to travel and spread the gospel message. One night, he had a crazy dream about Gentiles (non-Jewish people) being welcomed into God's kingdom just as much as any Jew. This was unheard-of at the time, because Jews and Gentiles didn't mix with each other. The Jewish people considered the Gentiles to be outside of God's plan of salvation, while many Gentiles in those days (and still today) hated and persecuted the Jewish people. But this vision of Peter's communicated that the Gentiles needed to hear the gospel as much as anybody else. The prophets spoke of a day when the whole world would come together to worship YHWH, the one true God of Israel. That time was now.

Not only was this message countercultural for Rome, but it was also countercultural for the Jews. It went against so many of their strong beliefs! From that day forward, Gentiles were invited to become the people of God as well.

To the Ends of the Earth

In Saul's time, Antioch was the largest city in that part of the world, and the church there was thriving. Jews and Gentiles were following Jesus and forming a true community of believers that loved and cared for each other. A leader of the Jerusalem church named Barnabas joined forces with Saul in Antioch to help their numbers grow even larger. The church decided it was time for them to send members of their congregation out to bring the gospel to the rest of the known Roman world. Barnabas and Saul would be the first missionaries.

Now Saul, who was a Jewish believer, had a very Jewish name. Since he was going to be preaching to Gentiles throughout the Roman world, he adopted his Roman name, Paul, from that time on.

On this first missionary journey, Paul and Barnabas went throughout Asia Minor (modern-day Turkey) sharing the good news that Jesus was King and the kingdom of God was here. Some cities welcomed their message, while others threw them out of town.

This journey led to more clashes with Jews than it did with Gentiles. Some Jewish people couldn't get over the idea that God would allow Gentiles into his plan. The Jews thought the Gentiles needed to convert to their religion, follow their laws, and even be circumcised, but Paul and Barnabas disagreed. The debate ended at a council meeting at the church in Jerusalem, where the consensus was that Gentiles didn't need to do anything physical to be accepted into the family of Jesus. They just needed to repent and obey Jesus' teachings. This was a defining moment in the church, and it paved the way for all that was to come.

Paul was sent out on a second missionary journey, this time alongside a man named Silas, and they went to start churches throughout Asia Minor and Greece. On this journey, they began to clash with the Greek and Roman worlds more than the Jewish worlds. These cities had their own gods to worship, but Paul was proclaiming that Jesus was King and only one true God existed: the God of Israel, YHWH. As you might guess, this didn't always go over well.

The gospel of Jesus contradicted the gospel of Rome. In Roman eyes, Caesar was the son of God, their lord and savior. And Caesar's gospel message was all about earthly power: violence, control, and might. You can imagine the confusion when Paul and Silas showed up in towns saying they had a new gospel—a message of good news—and that the new kingdom consisted of peace and love, not military power.

According to Roman thought, Caesar made the world a better place through his power—so all people needed to convert to their way of life.

But Paul and Silas taught that God's kingdom offered a much better way of living—a way of forgiveness, freedom, and peace.

The people had to decide: Who were they going to side with? Caesar or Jesus?

The Romans thought Paul and Silas were rebelling against the Roman Empire, so they were thrown in prison time and time again. But whenever they went to trial, it became clear to everyone that they weren't actual threats. Paul and Silas just didn't conform to the ways of society. Their refusal to conform was looked down upon (as it still can be today), but it was not illegal. At least, it was not worth serious imprisonment.

Paul was then sent out for his third missionary journey. He returned to a lot of the places he'd visited on his second journey, and he continued to build the churches in each area and teach them the ways of Jesus. This third journey ended back in Jerusalem, where he ran into even more resistance than he had experienced on his travels to other lands. The Jews weren't happy to have him back because they felt he was a traitor who had blasphemed the temple and the law.

The whole city went into an uproar, causing enough chaos for the city officials to get involved. Roman soldiers arrested Paul and brought him before the Roman governor Felix, then Festus, and eventually King Agrippa.

Everyone kept trying to convict Paul of different things, but none of the charges ever proved to be true. But just because he was innocent didn't mean he didn't do some serious jail time. In between trials, Paul spent a lot of time either alone in prison or under house arrest.

While Paul was under arrest, he used his time to write many letters to the different churches he had helped establish throughout the ancient world. These letters make up the majority of the New Testament, teaching readers what it means to live as followers of Jesus, and they still advise us today.

The book of Acts shows us what the early church dealt with and how they proceeded to spread the gospel around the world. As Christians today, our responsibility is to continue spreading the message of God's kingdom in every way possible.

One-Sentence Recap

The book of Acts details the spread of the gospel message from Jerusalem to Judea and Samaria, and then to "the ends of the earth."

How to Apply This Lesson to Your Life

As Christians, we should ask the Holy Spirit to give us the courage to share our faith even when we encounter resistance and persecution.

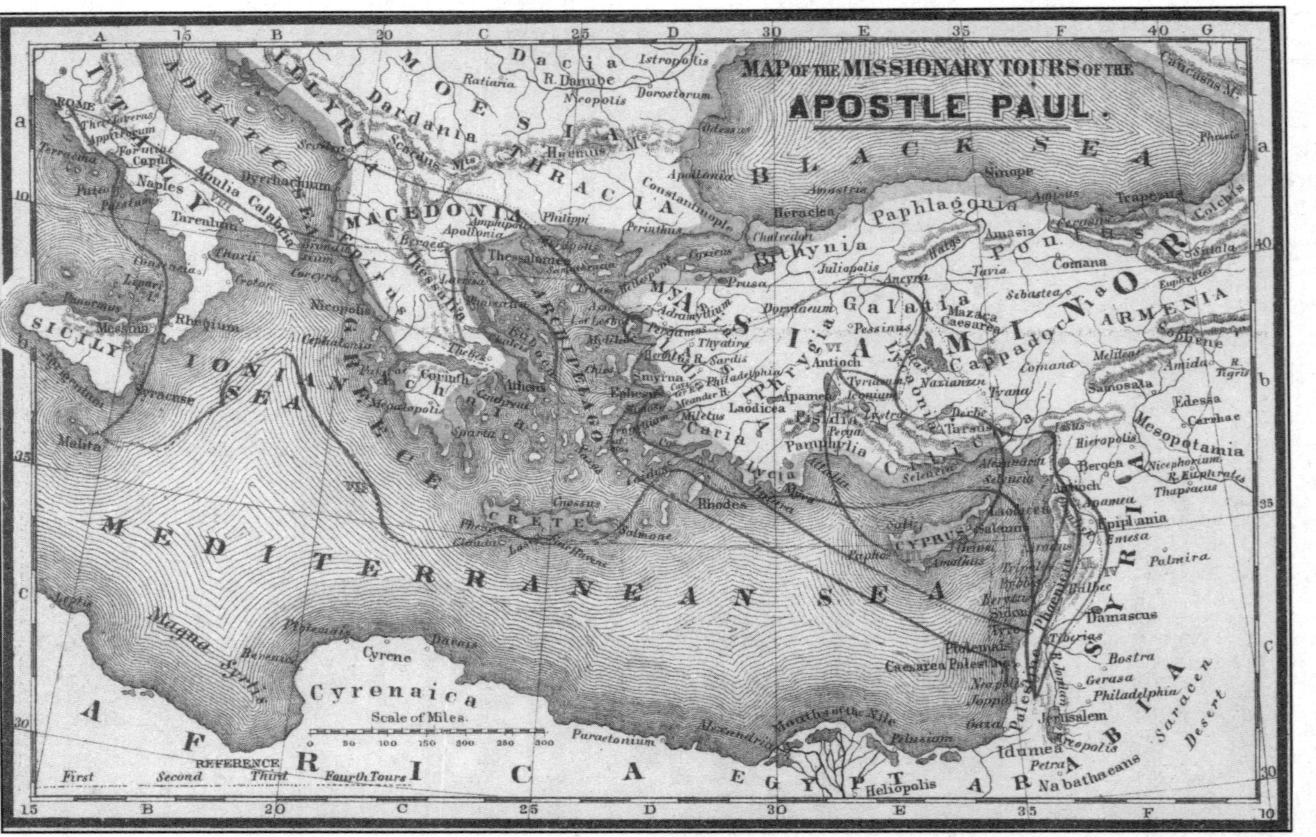

MAP OF THE MISSIONARY TOURS OF THE
APOSTLE PAUL.
BLACK SEA
MEDITERRANEAN SEA
IONIAN SEA
ARCHIPELAGO
ITALY
ROME
Naples
Tarentum
Apulia
Calabria
Rhegium
Messina
Syracuse
SICILY
Melita
ILLYRIA
Dyrrachium
MOESIA
Dardania
Dacia
R. Danube
Ratiaria
Nicopolis
Istropolis
Dorostorum
THRACIA
Constantinople
Apollonia
Philippi
Perinthus
MACEDONIA
Amphipolis
Thessalonica
Beroea
Epirus
Thessalia
Larissa
Nicopolis
Cephalonia
GRAECIA
Achaia
Corinth
Athens
Sparta
Megalopolis
Euboea
CRETE
Cnossus
Salmone
Rhodes
ASIA MINOR
MYSIA
Troas
Pergamus
Thyatira
Sardis
Smyrna
Philadelphia
Ephesus
Miletus
Caria
Laodicea
Lycia
Pisidia
Pamphylia
Perga
Phrygia
Antioch
Iconium
Lystra
Derbe
Tarsus
Cilicia
Seleucia
Bithynia
Chalcedon
Heraclea
Amastris
Juliopolis
Prusa
Dorylaeum
Galatia
Ancyra
Pessinus
Paphlagonia
Sinope
Amasia
Amisus
Pontus
Trapezus
Colchis
Phasis
Caucasus M.
Comana
Tavia
Sebastea
Mazaca
Caesarea
Cappadocia
Nazianzen
Tyana
ARMENIA
Sophene
Amida
R. Tigris
Samosata
Edessa
Carrhae
Mesopotamia
Hieropolis
Beroea
Nicephorium
R. Euphrates
Thapsacus
Antioch
Apamea
Epiphania
Emesa
Palmira
SYRIA
Balbec
Damascus
CYPRUS
Salamis
Paphos
Amathus
Phoenicia
Sidon
Tyre
Ptolemais
Caesarea Palestina
Joppa
Gaza
Palestine
R. Jordan
Tiberias
Jerusalem
Bostra
Gerasa
Philadelphia
Idumea
Petra
Nabathaeans
ARABIA
Saracen Desert
EGYPT
Mouths of the Nile
Alexandria
Pelusium
Heliopolis
Paraetonium
AFRICA
Cyrenaica
Cyrene
Magna Syrtis
Scale of Miles.
0 50 100 150 200 250 300
REFERENCE
First Second Third Fourth Tours

Chapter 35

Paul's Epistles

As Paul moved from city to city on his missionary journeys, he wrote letters to his former churches to answer questions and encourage them in their faith. The New Testament largely consists of Paul's letters, as well as letters written by Peter, John, James, and Jude to specific churches or specific people.

Paul's letters (or epistles, as some call them) can be split into three main groups: early letters to churches, late letters to churches, and letters to individuals.

Early Letters to Churches

The letters to the early churches are all named after the cities the letters were sent to. You'll see later that some letters are named after the individuals receiving the letters or who wrote them.

1 Thessalonians

One of the earliest letters Paul wrote was to the Thessalonians. The church in Thessalonica had a large Jewish population, so Paul had built a church there.

In any new city, Paul would begin by going to the local synagogue and walking the Jews through how Jesus was their promised hope, the continuation of their covenant with God. Whoever acknowledged Jesus as King—currently seated on the throne, ruling and reigning over the world—would become a new group of Jesus followers in that city. Then they would start their own thing, welcoming anybody who wanted to join.

After the first month in Thessalonica, Paul had to leave because of too much conflict with the Torah-observing Jews who disagreed about Jesus' role in the story. Also, tensions were mounting between the Roman authorities and these new "Christians" who were going against Caesar by saying they were part of a different kingdom with a better king. Same story, just different city.

Paul loved this church, so he sent his friend and protégé Timothy to check on them and help where needed. After Timothy confirmed their strength and dedication to the gospel, Paul wrote this letter to encourage them to press on through their persecution. He also responded to a few questions they'd been debating.

One of the questions the Thessalonians had was, What happens to Christians when they die? Paul shared with them that Jesus was the first to rise from the dead, and at his second coming all believers living and dead would meet him in the sky and welcome him back to earth, to restore everything once and for all. So Paul told them to maintain a kingdom perspective moving forward.

He reminded them that Jesus was still King, even though the persecution made it seem otherwise.

2 Thessalonians

Paul's second letter to the Thessalonians was written shortly after the first one. Timothy had told Paul that things in Thessalonica had taken a turn for the worse. The persecution was stronger than ever, and they had more and more questions about Jesus' second coming because some false teachings were being spread throughout the churches.

Remember, the Thessalonians didn't have a New Testament Bible or a collection of accepted doctrinal beliefs for what it meant to be a Christian. Any questions they had were answered through letters, by word of mouth, or directly by an apostle. The beginning stages of any new project can be confusing and difficult, and God's kingdom project was no different.

Paul addressed more questions about the end times. He put their anxiety to rest and encouraged them to press on, work hard, and share the good news of Jesus with those around them.

Galatians

Paul wrote Galatians to the churches in the region of Galatia, part of Asia Minor. The churches in Galatia were primarily composed of Gentile believers, but a group of Jewish leaders had come in saying that the Gentile Christians needed to observe the Jewish laws and customs. Paul didn't agree with the Jewish leaders. Even though he observed Jewish customs himself, he taught that Gentiles weren't subject to the same requirements.

This letter from Paul is intense. He was not happy at all with the Jewish leaders and the Gentiles who were listening to them. So with passion and holy anger, Paul cleared the air.

One of Paul's main arguments in this letter was that even though the law had a purpose for its time, it could not fully save anyone. The law led to a never-ending cycle of failure and repentance—but Jesus made a way. Faith in him was all one needed to be saved and be included in the family of God. Paul wrote about being "justified by faith"—how belief in Jesus made them "righteous" in God's eyes.

Likewise, you and I have been made right with God through faith in Jesus, and Jesus alone. We are now free from our sin! This was major news for the Galatians to be hearing.

And through this faith in Jesus and the Spirit working in our lives, we are becoming more and more like Jesus every day. Paul called it the fruit of the Spirit (Galatians 5:22–23). As we get closer to Jesus, we are filled with things like love, joy, peace, patience, kindness, goodness, faithfulness, gentleness, and self-control. These are the characteristics of a believer in Jesus. This is what it means to be a new creation.

Paul was clear in this letter: Christians were (and are) no longer tied to the old covenant, the law, but were freed from sin through Christ under the new covenant.

1 Corinthians

Paul wrote his next set of letters to the church in Corinth, which was a port city heavily influenced by Greek culture. The Corinthians had a bunch of temples and were known for their intellect, sophistication, and wealth. Paul knew that if he planted a successful church in this region, it would help spread the message of Jesus to many other parts of the ancient world.

But dealing with the Corinthians was much easier said than done.

Paul wrote this letter as something of a correction to many of their beliefs. Corinth was a big, busy, diverse city, so there were competing practices, philosophies, and cultures in the Corinthian church. It was a little chaotic. Paul did his best to help them, but you can sense his frustration in the letter.

So Paul encouraged them to go back to the basics, to the foundation of their faith. Jesus was crucified, but he rose from the dead—and now they had hope for the future, upon the completion of God's plan.

2 Corinthians

This second letter to the Corinthians was written because a group of false apostles was going from church to church, spreading lies about Paul. Paul wrote to correct the record: His faith was all about Jesus—nothing more, nothing less.

Paul recounted Jesus saying to him, "My grace is sufficient for you, for my power is perfected in weakness." Paul then said to the Corinthians, "Therefore, I will most gladly boast all the more about my weaknesses, so that Christ's power may reside in me. So I take pleasure in weaknesses, insults, hardships, persecutions, and in difficulties, for the sake of Christ. For when I am weak, then I am strong" (12:9–10).

Paul meant that Jesus was the one who needed to be exalted—not the people he used in the kingdom. This demanded a mindset shift. At the root of this letter, Paul was also showing the Corinthians how to deal with criticism and be unified as a church community.

Romans

The next letter Paul wrote was to the Christian believers in Rome. Rome was a wild place in the late AD 50s, when it was the beating heart of the known world. The church there was full of Jewish and Gentile followers of Jesus, but the tensions between the Jews and Jewish Christians was rising.

Claudius, the Roman emperor of the time, actually kicked all of the Jews out of Rome because their fights about Jesus were getting so disruptive. So the Jews and Jewish Christians all had to leave Rome, but the Gentile believers were allowed to stay. Five years later, when the Jewish Christians came back into the city, they found a significant change in the way the Gentile believers were running the church. These changes caused even more of a division between the two communities.

So Paul wrote his magnum opus: the book of Romans. He explained the gospel message to both Jewish believers and Gentile believers, in hopes of creating unity under Christ and Christ alone. This letter is Paul's masterpiece—his announcement that Jesus was the good news and that he had receipts to back it up. He wrote about sin and salvation and judgment and justification by faith and grace and living in harmony with one another, both Jewish and Gentile believers in Jesus alike. The letter has shaped the doctrine of Christianity for two thousand years.

Late Letters to Churches

Whenever Paul entered into a new city, some people liked him and some people hated him. And often, the people who hated him had louder voices than the others, resulting in backlash from the Roman authorities. Pressure grew and persecution grew along with it, landing Paul in jail cells in multiple cities, including Caesarea, Rome, and possibly others.

Paul was a Roman citizen, which meant he received slightly better accommodations than other prisoners. But prison was still prison, and he was still being tried for various "crimes," usually for causing chaos and speaking against Caesar, the lord and savior of the Romans.

Three of the letters Paul wrote while in prison (most likely in Rome, but possibly Ephesus as well) were Ephesians, Philippians, and Colossians. These are known as the Prison Epistles. Though written amid less-than-ideal scenarios, Paul's letters encouraged the churches to persevere in faith.

Ephesians

The first letter Paul wrote was to the church in Ephesus, which wasn't necessarily one specific church but a regional cluster of churches that would have passed around this letter. Ephesus was the third-largest city in the ancient world, behind Rome and Alexandria. Commerce was booming, and as a port city connecting the East to the West, it would have been very ethnically and culturally diverse.

Ephesus was well-known for its pagan temples and religious life, dedicated to all sorts of Greek and Roman gods, with the Temple of Artemis—one of the Seven Wonders of the Ancient World—being the most important. Everything in Ephesus was built around Artemis. This was the landscape in which Paul was writing, after spending a few years there building a thriving community of Jesus followers.

Paul taught that the church is the body of Christ, with Jesus as the head. We are not the evangelical body or the Catholic body or the apostolic body. We are all one body: the church. We are meant to be one, united for the same cause. We have all been saved by our faith in Jesus, not our works. So Paul spent time in the first part of this letter discussing how the followers of Jesus could get along better with other believers. He also discussed the different and important roles people were to play. He explained that one person might be an ear in the body, and another might be the nose—but each part needed the other to function properly as one body. The ear couldn't just decide it didn't need the nose; no part could decide it just didn't need its fellow believers. In the church, Paul wrote, everyone needed each other.

Paul discussed how Jesus' followers were in a spiritual battle with various forces of evil, much more than a physical battle with the Roman government. So Paul encouraged the believers to put on a metaphorical "armor of God" every day to fight those battles.

The book of Ephesians is a great starting point for people who want to dive into the letters of Paul.

Philippians

Paul wrote his next letter to the church in Philippi, which he founded during his second missionary journey. Philippi was a smaller city than Ephesus, but it was significant due to its location on the Via Egnatia, one of the major highways connecting Rome in the West to the regions of the East. Philippi was a Roman colony full of military veterans, known for its patriotism.

The Philippians were the definition of pledged allegiance to Rome. Paul was quite a rebel in the sense that he called people to follow Jesus instead of Caesar.

But this letter of Paul's was full of joy. Even though he was in prison, and even though the Philippians were persecuted, the joy of the Lord was a testimony to the work that Jesus was doing in their lives.

Paul commanded them: "Rejoice in the Lord always. I will say it again: Rejoice!" He went on to say, "Whatever is true, whatever is honorable, whatever is just, whatever is pure, whatever is lovely, whatever is commendable—if there is any moral excellence and if there is anything praiseworthy—dwell on these things" (Philippians 4:4, 8).

Paul called the Philippians (and us) to imitate the life of Jesus in all they did and to continue spreading the good news of Jesus Christ.

Colossians

The third letter Paul wrote to a church while in prison was to the Christian community in Colossae, a small city that was influenced by Greek and Roman thought. Colossae wasn't a thriving city by any means—it was more like a rural town than a multicultural epicenter like Rome or Ephesus—but Paul explained their faith so they wouldn't be confused by all the other religious beliefs in the surrounding communities. The Colossians were influenced not only by the worship of Greek and Roman gods but also by the Gnosticism that was most likely beginning to spread around this time.

Gnosticism is the belief that the physical world and spiritual world are two completely different things that don't blend at all. The physical was evil, while the spiritual was good and pure. Gnostics essentially believed that salvation came from increasing their knowledge of the divine and condemning their bodies (which were physical and therefore evil).

Paul tried to clear the air for them and encourage them to keep growing closer to Jesus.

Paul also encouraged the Colossians to live in a way unique to Christ. This meant letting go of the way things were and adapting to the new ways of Jesus. Paul described the transformation as taking off your old self and putting on the new self (Colossians 3:9–10). There was no longer Gentile or Jew, circumcised or uncircumcised, slave or free; they were now a new creation and part of a new humanity, a collective of kingdom people. As such, he encouraged them to act like it—to view all of life through the lens of Jesus.

Paul's letters to the Ephesians, Philippians, and Colossians teach us what it means to live as part of the new creation, new humanity, and new kingdom Jesus incorporated with his death and resurrection.

Letters to Individuals

The final letters from the apostle Paul were written to individuals. Three of these letters (1 Timothy, 2 Timothy, and Titus) are considered the Pastoral Epistles, while the fourth letter (Philemon) is more like a letter of recommendation.

1 Timothy

When Paul met Timothy in Lystra, he could sense the fire burning within him for the Scriptures. He asked Timothy to follow him, to help him spread the gospel message of Jesus around the world.

So after years of following Paul, Timothy was sent on his own missionary journeys around the ancient world, to check in on churches as Paul's representative. When Timothy arrived, it was as if the authority of Paul was there.

Paul sent Timothy to oversee the church at Ephesus for a while because of the spreading of false doctrine. Timothy's job was to clear up any confusion and bring order to the church, and to teach them how to properly live out their faith.

After some time, Paul sent Timothy a letter. This letter is considered a Pastoral Epistle because of its advice to Timothy on how to pastor and organize the church. This meant making sure the people had correct theology.

Paul wrote, "Instruct them to do what is good, to be rich in good works, to be generous and willing to share" (1 Timothy 6:18). Paul wanted Christians to be a positive influence on their community, to love others into the kingdom instead of condemning them for believing something different. This was a strategy of inclusion and love. Everyone was welcome in the kingdom of God.

If you are a pastor (or want to be one day), this letter provides many relevant and helpful tools.

2 Timothy

We aren't sure how much time passed between Paul's first and second letters to Timothy, but we know Paul's situation had changed drastically. He was now in prison in Rome, and from his perspective, things weren't looking good. Paul wrote this letter while under the impression that his time was growing short.

So Paul's second and final letter to Timothy was a very personal missive that seems strange to us to read in the Bible. Paul knew he was about to die, and he asked Timothy to come spend the winter with him as a final farewell before his death. He was all alone and wanted a friend with him for his final few days on earth.

Paul also encouraged Timothy to remain steadfast in his faith and continue fighting the good fight. No matter the challenges headed his way, they would all be worth it in light of Jesus. He said, "If we died with him, we will also live with him; if we endure, we will also reign with him; if we deny him, he will also deny us; if we are faithless, he remains faithful, for he cannot deny himself" (2 Timothy 2:11–13). Everything they did was for Jesus, no matter what suffering came their way.

The message they were spreading together was worth it.

Before Timothy made his way to Rome, Paul encouraged him to put leaders in place who would remain faithful to the gospel message and stand up against the false teachers that continued to infiltrate their churches. Then Paul told him to come quickly and to bring a coat he had left in Troas, along with his scrolls and parchments. Though we often overlook the fact that these letters were written by and to real people at real times, these simple housekeeping items help humanize Paul, Timothy, and other early Christian leaders.

Titus

Paul's other main disciple was a guy named Titus who had helped Paul in many cities during his missionary journeys. Paul trusted Titus and knew he was up for whatever Paul asked him to do, such as staying to help organize a church in one of the roughest areas of the ancient world, an island off the coast of Greece called Crete.

Crete was a dangerous place. Paul quoted one of the Cretan prophets who said, "Cretans are always liars, evil beasts, lazy gluttons" (Titus 1:12). The stereotypical Cretan was violent, immoral, and not to be trusted. As far as Paul was concerned, that just meant they were the perfect people to be influenced by the gospel message of Jesus. Paul knew that if he could give the Cretans a purpose, something to live for, they would be just as passionate for godly things as they were for ungodly things.

So Paul sent Titus to Crete to put the church in line. He wrote this letter to teach Titus how to organize the church with elders and deacons. He also taught him what to do with the false teachers.

It's a short, practical letter telling Titus how to turn things around and build a thriving church community. Paul focused a lot on the importance of doing good in light of the gospel. Doing good wouldn't save them, but doing good was the *result* of their salvation. Their lifestyle must reflect their message. And as they were personally transformed, the rest of Crete would be transformed in the overflow of their actions.

Philemon

The fourth personal letter Paul wrote was more like a letter of recommendation for a guy named Onesimus. It's one of the shortest letters in the New Testament and seems very random unless you understand its context.

There was a wealthy man named Philemon who most likely became a follower of Jesus at the church in Ephesus. He met Paul there, and then later he became a leader in the Colossian church. Philemon had a slave named Onesimus who had wronged him somehow and then run away.

We aren't sure how Onesimus ended up in prison with Paul, but we do know that Onesimus became a follower of Jesus and a helper to Paul in prison.

There was a problem though. Paul couldn't handle knowing that Onesimus had wronged his friend. So Paul wrote this letter to Philemon, asking him to forgive Onesimus and bring him back into his family—not as a slave but as a brother in Christ. The punishment for a runaway slave was supposed to be death, so Paul's request was extremely countercultural. But that was the upside-down kingdom of God. Things were different in the new kingdom, and one of the main virtues was (and is) forgiveness.

We don't know exactly what happened when Onesimus delivered the letter to Philemon, but church tradition tells us that Onesimus became a bishop in Ephesus and spent his life spreading the gospel message of Jesus. All thanks to Paul.

That wraps up our look at the letters of Paul. In the next chapter, we'll tackle the General Epistles.

One-Sentence Recap

Paul wrote a collection of letters to show believers what to do within their churches, and to encourage them to keep the gospel of Jesus their main focus by living it out each day.

How to Apply This Lesson to Your Life

As followers of Jesus, and potentially leaders within our church communities, we need to focus on sound doctrine and living as reflections of Jesus as we grow closer to him.

Chapter 36

The General Epistles

The rest of the New Testament consists of letters that weren't written by Paul. Some of them were written by Jesus' disciples Peter and John. Some were written by James and Jude, Jesus' half brothers. And one was written by a mystery author. These books are known as the General Epistles.

Peter's Epistles

Peter's name was originally Simon, meaning "reed." He could be blown in the wind. But Jesus renamed him Peter, which means "rock," because it was upon Peter that Jesus would build his church. Peter's relationship with Jesus was a roller coaster, and Peter himself was an impulsive guy. Sometimes he was all in; sometimes he doubted; sometimes he said the right thing; and sometimes he should have kept his mouth shut. But he was exactly the kind of guy Jesus could use as the foundation of the church, and at the end of the day, Peter was faithful and committed to spreading God's kingdom. Remember how we learned that Paul was like an Ivy Leaguer? Peter would have been on the other end of the academic spectrum. God used both types of people to build his kingdom, just as he does today.

As the early church grew, Peter left Jerusalem and began preaching throughout Judea and Samaria, eventually landing in Rome to help grow the church there. Rome was obviously the epicenter of the Roman Empire, so whatever began there was most likely to spread throughout the rest of the ancient world. So as the persecution of Christians became popular in Rome, persecution trended throughout the empire.

It was a devastating time for Christians, who were living under constant threat. Peter knew this persecution would eventually spread to the other parts of the Roman world, which is why he decided to write these two letters in the first place.

1 Peter

Peter wrote the first letter to a group of churches in northern Asia Minor, which is modern-day Turkey. We don't have records of Peter living there, but we know he was somewhat of a leader to these churches and highly respected among them.

Peter was basically saying to the members of the church, "Get ready, because the persecution is going to get even worse." They were already suffering for their faith, but they hadn't seen anything yet. Yet this was a letter of hope to them, encouraging believers to persevere.

When suffering increases, the most important thing is to have a faith that can't be shaken. Instead of focusing on their present suffering, Peter wanted his readers to set their hearts on the future—so that no matter what happened, they would know where they were going to end up.

Peter emphasized Christian identity, saying, "You are a chosen race, a royal priesthood, a holy nation, a people for his possession, so that you may proclaim the praises of the one who called you out of darkness into his marvelous light" (1 Peter 2:9). The only interaction some people would have with the living God was through them, so Peter wanted the audience to know their worth and to remain confident that God was using them to positively impact the world.

2 Peter

Peter's second letter was written shortly after the first letter, to the same region in Asia Minor. While the first letter was focused on persecution from outsiders, this letter was directed inward. Different heresies were spreading throughout the churches, and Peter wanted to squash them before they took root.

Peter could sense that his own martyrdom was right around the corner, and he knew these heresies and false teachings would only increase once he was no longer alive. The generation of people who had personally walked and talked with Jesus was starting to die out, which meant they had to do everything possible to make sure their eyewitness testimonies trumped the lies, misunderstandings, and heresies that were springing up about who Jesus was. And praise God that Peter wrote this letter when he did, because soon after, he was crucified for his faith.

Through both letters, Peter's message is consistent: hope. The churches needed hope for the future and confidence in where God's plan of redemption was heading. One day we will be on the new earth, where sin will be removed and all will be right in the world. So what do we do between now and then? Remain hopeful, love like Jesus, focus on righteousness, and grow in faith.

Hebrews

The letter to the Hebrews (another name for Jewish people) can be a confusing letter to Gentile Christians. Many people don't understand the importance of certain aspects of the law and what the Old Testament provided for Jewish people. But not you. You've spent the last thirty-five chapters digging deep into the text. This letter is all about how Jesus is the better version of everything the audience once relied on. It's an argument for the superiority of Jesus over the older way of doing things.

The author encouraged readers to leave their traditions and rules behind in order to focus on Jesus alone.

Speaking of the author, who wrote it?

This is a big question mark for scholars today. Early church tradition contended that Paul was the author, but scholars no longer think that is the case. Now one of the most common theories is that it was written by one of Paul's coworkers. Some people think a guy named Barnabas wrote it. Others think it may have been written by another influential early Christian named Apollos. Still others think Apollos's wife, Priscilla—herself an influential early Christian—may have penned it. We just don't know for sure.

Regardless of who the author was, the focus of the letter to the Hebrews was that Jesus was "better." The old way of doing faith had passed away, and the new had arrived in the life of Jesus, the Son of God, the Messiah.

So instead of falling back into their old ways of doing things, believers were encouraged by the author of Hebrews to carry on through their persecution and remain faithful to Jesus, who had initiated a completely new covenant that was better than anything they could've imagined.

The Letters of James and Jude

Can you imagine what it would've been like to be the half brother of Jesus?

When Jesus began his ministry, the Bible says his brothers and family were skeptical and didn't follow him at first. Only after Jesus' resurrection did they become his disciples.

James and Jude were two of Jesus' four brothers, and they actually wrote two pretty unique letters that we have in our New Testament today.

James

James addressed his letter to the "twelve tribes [of Israel] dispersed abroad"—the Jewish believers who had been scattered all over the ancient world (1:1).

Once Peter left the church in Jerusalem to go about his own missionary journeys, he placed the church in the hands of James to carry on the legacy and expand the church body. Who better to lead the early church than the guy who had grown up alongside Jesus, right?

The Jerusalem church was the original church, and as you can imagine, its members received a lot of backlash for their beliefs. Many Jews weren't crazy about all these people saying the Messiah had come. So the Jerusalem church was persecuted for years and years. James himself was stoned to death in AD 62.

But amid the persecution and hard times, James believed God was good and had a purpose for the suffering. So James wrote a letter that's quite different from other New Testament letters. It's more like the book of Proverbs mixed with a little Jesus and his kingdom than a letter addressing a specific problem. James pulled a bunch of topics and sayings from Jesus' Sermon on the Mount in hopes of leading the Jewish Christian community in godly wisdom.

James didn't take it easy on his readers. This book has a lot more "tough talk" than most of the New Testament, as James hoped to convict his readers so they might change and live more Jesus-centered lifestyles. The kingdom of God was a new way of looking at things, and those who really believed it would live it out. James called some early believers out for saying they believed one thing while living another way. He encouraged his audience to make sure their day-to-day actions lived up to their beliefs.

Jude

The letter of Jude is a very short epistle written by Jesus' other brother, Jude (or Judah in Hebrew). After the resurrection of Jesus, Jude became known as a missionary throughout the ancient world, as he taught all about his brother. As a Jewish Christian himself, Jude was writing to a very Jewish audience who had a firm understanding of Hebrew Scripture. We don't know which city they were in specifically, but we know these believers dealt with false teachers who claimed that since Jesus had saved them from their sins, they could live immorally in their community.

Jude wasn't having any of it. Just because they were saved didn't mean they could do whatever they wanted. Jesus calls us to live at even higher standards now.

So Jude wrote a short letter, encouraging believers to stand firm in their faith and contend for what they believed in. "Go back to the basics," he told them. "You know what is and isn't right."

He warned the audience that if they kept traveling down the wrong path, they would end up like other groups of rebels in the Old Testament. He wrote about the Israelites in the wilderness, disobeying God's commands. His point was that chasing after the sexual immorality of the Roman world would only lead to destruction. They were meant to live holy lives, not just repeating the same sins they had repented of. It didn't work like that.

Faithfulness to Jesus was of utmost importance to Jude. And the way we live as Christians is the greatest reflection of our beliefs.

John's Epistles

The spread of Gnosticism during the early church period played a large role in pulling people away from their faith. Remember, Gnosticism taught that growing in knowledge was the way to salvation and that anything spiritual was good, while anything physical was bad. This binary went against everything the apostles were saying, because they believed Jesus was both 100 percent God and 100 percent man at the same time—and it was through him alone that salvation was possible.

So a division was growing within the church, as leaders with a Gnostic view were spreading lies about Jesus and whether he'd actually risen from the dead.

For us as Christians, the resurrection is the crux of our beliefs. If Jesus didn't rise from the dead in his physical body, then everything he said about being the Messiah was a lie.

But he did.

And it's this physical resurrection that gives us hope for the future, as Jesus was the first to be resurrected while the rest of us wait for our time at the second coming.

So as all this debate was taking place around the ancient world, John—the disciple whom Jesus loved—was getting older and now overseeing the house churches around Ephesus. He wrote three little letters encouraging them to grow in their faith, to persevere through persecution, and to combat false teachings.

The first letter was more like a poem or a sermon that could be passed around from one church to the next to be read in front of the congregations. The second and third letters were most likely "cover letters" to be given in addition to the main letter.

1 John

The first letter John wrote to the churches was directly related to the false accusations about Jesus. John confirmed who Jesus really was: the long-awaited Jewish Messiah who was God in the flesh.

John needed to remind them of the teachings of Jesus and to boost their confidence in the testimonies of people who knew and saw Jesus after he rose from the dead. The Gnostics argued that Jesus may have been *spiritually* resurrected, but he never *physically* resurrected. John argued that not only had he himself seen the resurrected Jesus in the flesh but hundreds of other early believers had as well.

John was very black-and-white in the way he approached his messages. He wrote that we walk in either light or darkness.

God is light, and as believers in the sacrifice of Jesus—and as those who now have victory over sin and death—we must also focus on shining that light in the world. What does that mean?

To know God and obey his commands to bring heaven to earth.

The second topic John focused on was God as love.

He said that as children of God, our responsibility and role is to love God and love others. Love is the greatest evidence of a relationship with Jesus. Love is a verb, not a feeling. Love is what you do.

According to John, God *is* love. So the light and love of God change everything.

2 John

As I mentioned, the second and third letters of John seem to be like cover letters to the first letter. They're much shorter and addressed to specific people, and 2 John was addressed to "the elect lady and her children."

Different teachers traveled from city to city at the time, just as we saw Paul and Peter doing in earlier chapters. This was a great occurrence when the message was in line with Jesus, but some Gnostic teachers were traveling as well. Without Bibles to base their beliefs on, churches didn't always know whom to trust.

John wrote this short letter to a specific house church to warn them that false teachers were on their way. He explained that the main way to tell if someone was trustworthy was to determine whether they believed Jesus was the Messiah in the flesh.

3 John

The third and final letter from John is very similar to the second one in that it talks about hospitality and how to treat certain people. It's a very personal letter, and reading it feels like reading someone's mail. John wrote this letter to a man named Gaius, encouraging him in his hospitality and dedication to the truth of the gospel of Jesus Christ.

John said to continue showing hospitality to believers who agreed on the same doctrines. He also told Gaius not to listen to Diotrephes, a leader in the church who disagreed with John and didn't want people to support any traveling preachers (including the good ones). John wrote that Diotrephes was just being prideful and "spreading malicious nonsense" (v. 10 NIV).

John went on to say, "Do not imitate what is evil, but what is good. The one who does good is of God; the one who does evil has not seen God" (v. 11).

These letters for the early church can still encourage us today. The writers continue instructing us on how to combat false teachers and focus on bringing the kingdom of God everywhere we go—through the love and light of Jesus.

One-Sentence Recap

The General Epistles were meant to combat false teachers who were spreading a gospel contrary to Jesus, but they also focused on the importance of love and obedience in light of Jesus' new covenant.

How to Apply This Lesson to Your Life

If we want to be more like Jesus, we need to view life from his perspective and be reflections of him to our communities. How can we be more loving to those around us? How can we be lights in the darkness? How can we reflect him in all we do?

Part Nine

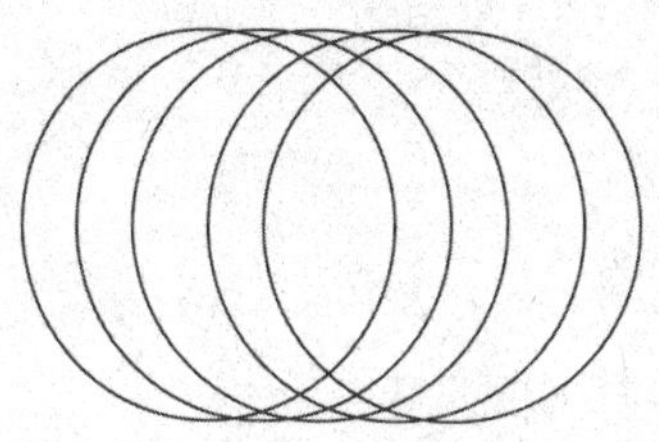

THE END TIMES

Chapter 37

Understanding Revelation

What do you think about when you hear the word *apocalyptic*?

The end of the world?

Running out of food at the grocery store?

People in line for gas?

Zombies?

The book of Revelation coming to life?

Yeah, same.

But that's not what the word means at all. *Apocalypse* in Greek means "to uncover or reveal." It's to have our eyes opened to something we couldn't see before.

In ancient Jewish thought, apocalypticism was a worldview that meant everything in life had two sides to it: good or evil. And it was up to you to decide which side you were on. Did you want to partner with God, the good side? Or did you want to partner with Satan, the evil side? And from there, this choice would impact everything you did in life. You chose one side, and then everything else trickled down from there.

Out of this worldview came a type of literature that was very popular at the time, called apocalyptic literature. You can find it in parts of Daniel, Ezekiel, Isaiah, Revelation, and a bunch of nonbiblical texts as well. Apocalyptic literature was a way for a prophet to describe what was happening in the spiritual realm in light of the readers' current circumstances, showing them a snapshot of the end result. It was a way of encouraging those who dealt with unprecedented persecution for their faith, to show them how God would eventually show up and win the battle on their behalf. Believers needed to persist in their faith, not give in to despair, because God would one day intervene and destroy the forces of evil once and for all.

Apocalyptic literature was meant to provide hope.

Many Christians are afraid to read these books. They're scary. They're strange. They're a little confusing. And yet, by not reading them we miss out on such an important part of God's story!

Yes, things are bad and sin runs rampant. The early Christians faced the constant threat of being thrown in jail or even executed for their faith. But apocalyptic literature showed them that things were going to be all right in the end. God was victorious, good was going to win, and his kingdom would reign supreme. One day the pain and struggles experienced on this earth would be replaced with a whole new earth, containing only God's presence.

Let's look at the book of Revelation as an example.

Maybe a pastor or your aunt or someone you trust has told you we are living during "the times of Revelation" or that "these are the end times." They want you to know that the rapture is coming, and things are only going to get darker from here.

That is one interpretation of the book.

But it's important to remember that people have been saying that we are in the end times since Jesus ascended to heaven. Different sects of Christianity have literally been debating for two thousand years when and how the end times will play out. And nobody has been right about it yet.

Are we living in the end times? Yes.

Could Jesus come back tomorrow? Yes.

Could Jesus come back two thousand years from now? Yes.

We can't get so caught up in turning the book of Revelation into a timetable that we miss out on the message of the text. Revelation was written to real people in real places dealing with real persecution, and it was written to give them hope for the future. We can pull so much out of it, but if our interpretations fail to bring us closer to Jesus in worship, we have missed the point completely. Just as many people of Jesus' day got so obsessed with interpreting *when* the Messiah was coming that they missed out on the real thing right in front of them, we can miss out on the true message of Revelation. When we focus on predicting a mysterious future, we miss out on what it has for us right here, right now, regardless of when Jesus is coming back.

For example, did you know that the book of Revelation has over four hundred allusions to the Old Testament?

And here we are as New Testament Christians thinking we can just read the book, compare it to the latest news headlines, and make sense of it all. That's how you get false doctrines. If we want to understand this style of literature, we must look backward first and consider the texts John was alluding to. That's how we find the deeper meaning behind the text.

I'm going to give you a short overview of the book and a few keys to help you understand it better, but I encourage you to study Revelation on your own at some point.

The book of Revelation is one long vision given to the apostle John while he was exiled on the island of Patmos, most likely for sharing his faith. At the beginning of the book, John wrote that it was a revelation, that it was a prophecy, and that it was apocalyptic. That meant the events he was about to share were from a divine perspective, not his own.

In this vision, a loud voice told John to write down all he saw and give it to the churches in seven different cities: Ephesus, Smyrna, Pergamum, Thyatira, Sardis, Philadelphia, and Laodicea. These churches were all clustered in Asia Minor and were dealing with increased persecution from Rome. Each one was handling this persecution differently. Rome was controlling the world's politics and economy and was forcing people to worship their gods and emperor, just as we saw in the past. This vision was meant to help the churches persevere, gain perspective, and withstand the pressure.

John quoted Jesus in his gospel, saying, "If the world hates you, keep in mind that it hated me first. If you belonged to the world, it would love you as its own. As it is, you do not belong to the world, but I have chosen you out of the world. That is why the world hates you" (John 15:18–19 NIV). The readers were living this out in the flesh, and it was only getting harder for them.

They believed the "world" to be the evil forces controlling things around them. Many had started to see Rome as the main villain at the time of John's writing, but the villain had been Babylon and Egypt before Rome, and it would surely be another world power in the future. To John, the world itself was the evil force, the enemy of God. And God, the one true God of Israel, was the good force who would one day claim total victory and take over.

So in the vision, John saw Jesus, who told him to let the churches know what he saw as hope for the present, in addition to what was going to happen at the end of the world as we know it. Jesus would show John the future, the "unveiling" of what was to come. Jesus wanted John and the churches to know that even though the world seemed to be falling apart, God would be victorious and would one day bring heaven to earth completely. The whole message is victory over evil.

John was then taken in his vision to the heavenly throne room where Jesus was the exalted king of the world. He saw twenty-four elders (twelve patriarchs and twelve apostles), the seven spirits of God, and the four living creatures (the same vision Daniel saw in his Old Testament book), worshipping Jesus day and night, saying, "Holy, holy, holy, Lord God, the Almighty, who was, who is, and who is to come" (Revelation 4:8).

This is happening right now, today, in real time. The echo of heaven is currently filled with praise and worship of God. He is on the throne, victorious over the Evil One on earth below. By starting the vision with this image, readers see that God is in control, even when our situations may suggest something different.

But in the vision, Jesus didn't look like a king. He was shown as a bloody lamb, symbolizing the perfect sacrificial lamb we talked about in Exodus and Passover. He was crucified for the sins of the world, as the ultimate offering for everyone. Jesus' resurrection was more than coming back from the dead; it was actually his enthronement in heaven.

As the praising continued, John explained a three-part series of seven cycles: Seven seals. Seven trumpets. Seven bowls. Each one a judgment upon the evil of the world.

This is the section where many people start to lose their cool a little. Debates flare up, weird conspiracies spread, and readers get scared for the future because they have been told this sequence of events will happen at the end times. And if you start believing that you're definitely living in the end times, then it's easy to start getting paranoid.

Now the idea that these things symbolize stuff that will happen in the end times is one theory, and this theory could be true. Another way to look at these things is as symbols for events that have already begun and will continue to happen until the return of Jesus, as part of an ongoing battle between good and evil.

We don't know for sure how to interpret these symbols. No matter how you look at it, this part of Revelation was meant to connect the original reader with the plagues from the exodus (remember those?) and show them how God would judge the unrighteous for persecuting his people.

The Seven Seals

First seal: A rider on a white horse was given a crown and went across the earth conquering his enemies.
Second seal: A rider on a red horse caused war among the people.
Third seal: A rider on a black horse brought famine.
Fourth seal: A rider on a pale horse named Death killed a quarter of the earth's population.
Fifth seal: Those who had been martyred were found on the altar crying out for justice.
Sixth seal: There was a great earthquake, the sun turned black, the moon turned red, and chaos broke out among the people.
Seventh seal: There was silence in heaven as the angel prepared for the seven trumpets.

The Seven Trumpets

First trumpet: Hail and fire fell on the earth, burning one third of the trees.
Second trumpet: A burning mountain was thrown into the sea, turning it to blood, and killing one-third of sea life.

Third trumpet: A star called Wormwood fell into the rivers and springs, causing many to die of thirst.
Fourth trumpet: Darkness fell on one-third of the sun, moon, and stars.
Fifth trumpet: Locusts were released, tormenting everyone who wasn't marked by Christ.
Sixth trumpet: Four angels were released to kill one-third of mankind.
Seventh trumpet: The heavens rejoiced as the kingdom of God defeated the kingdom of the world.

The Seven Bowls

First bowl: Sores broke out on everyone who had the Mark of the Beast.
Second bowl: The sea turned to blood and killed everything in it.
Third bowl: The rivers turned to blood.
Fourth bowl: The sun heated up and burned people.
Fifth bowl: The kingdom of the world was thrown into darkness.
Sixth bowl: The Euphrates River dried up, and the battle of Armageddon began.
Seventh bowl: A voice from heaven shouted, "It is done!" and a major storm wiped out everyone that was still alive.

You see? Revelation can be confusing. And definitely a little scary.

John's vision then featured a cosmic battle taking place between God and Satan, the people of God and the people of the world, angels and demons, good and evil.

Now let's talk about the Mark of the Beast.

People love speculating about who the antichrist is and what the Mark of the Beast will one day be. People also love to accuse this or that world leader, some politician or celebrity, of being the antichrist—and their accusations often include all sorts of theories about the Mark of the Beast.

There's a lot we don't know about this part of Revelation, but let me show you something interesting. In Judaism, there is a prayer that is said every morning and every night called the *Shema*. The prayer comes from Deuteronomy 6:4–5, which says, "Listen, Israel: The LORD our God, the LORD is one. Love the LORD your God with all your heart, with all your soul, and with all your strength."

Every day. Morning and night.

God had commanded his people to make the Torah their lives. To revolve every part of themselves around his commands. He told them to tie the commands as symbols to their hands and to bind them on their foreheads, all to show their allegiance to God.

Revelation 13:16–17 says, "[The beast] also forced all people, great and small, rich and poor, free and slave, to receive a mark on their right hands or on their foreheads, so that they could not buy or sell unless they had the mark, which is the name of the beast or the number of its name" (NIV). The text goes on to say that the number of its name was 666.

In Hebrew, each letter is associated with a number—an idea called *gemetria*.

Take the name Caesar Nero, for example. He had led the charge of persecution for many of these original readers a few decades prior, and as it turned out, the numbers of his name totaled up to 666, just as John said: "the number of its name."

The early Christians' main enemies were Rome and the Caesars, who were persecuting them for their beliefs. As believers, they were marked by God. And if they remained faithful to God, the persecution continued—including forms of discrimination, such as Christians not being allowed to buy and sell in Rome.

So according to John, this Mark of the Beast was anti-*Shema*, something that dedicated its people to another power that wasn't God. In other words, the readers of Revelation would have understood this Mark of the Beast as relevant to their lives there and then, not necessarily as some prediction of something that might happen in the future. And John was giving them a choice of who they would follow: the God of Israel or the evil forces controlling the world.

That's just one example, but story after story, symbol after symbol, seal after seal, this vision John had was all about how one day everyone who opposes God will be judged. Then God will finally be victorious over the Evil One.

The book of Revelation is meant to inspire hope in the reader, not fear.

Jesus ended the vision by saying, "Yes, I am coming soon." And we, as the modern reader, can still hold on to that hope ourselves. We already know how the end of history will play out. Jesus, the slain Passover Lamb, the risen King, the Lord of lords, has already defeated death, hell, and the grave. Every kingdom in the spirit of Babylon will one day bow to him. And one day he will come back for us, the church, at which point he will usher in a new heaven and new earth for us to spend eternity alongside him, redeemed, and back to our original calling from the garden.

In the next two chapters we will look at the final battle, hell, and the new heaven and new earth (which is most likely different from what you were taught growing up).

One-Sentence Recap

Jesus is already on the throne as the eternal King, and one day he will defeat the evil forces of this world for good.

How to Apply This Lesson to Your Life

This book should inspire us to be hopeful and faithful, no matter how intense the world may become. We are marked by God, not by Satan—and all our choices should reflect that.

Chapter 38

Judgment and Hell

What happens after we die?

Is hell a real place?

How could a good God send someone to hell for eternity?

Your view of the end times and what happens after Jesus returns impacts every part of your life whether you realize it or not.

Every religion has a different view of what happens at the end and where we go afterward. As Christians, our views should be shaped by Scripture, even if Scripture is hard to digest sometimes. We don't get to pick and choose which portions of the text we align with. You are either all in or out. It's as simple as that.

The Second Coming of Jesus

Thanks to the biblical account of the end times, we have hope that Jesus will one day return. When he does, he will get rid of evil completely and finish the restoration process of the world by incorporating the new heaven and new earth, along with a newly redeemed and resurrected body for each of us.

When Jesus returns, the whole world will know it. He will be seen in the sky, descending on a white horse, showing victory over the evil forces of the world. He will come to reign from the transformed earth, no longer on his throne in heaven. Instead, he'll rule from right here, where heaven and earth are finally joined back together. We'll talk about that more in the next chapter.

In the Roman world, when a victorious emperor would return home, the citizens would go out to meet him, welcoming him and walking with him back into the city. We have been given a similar image for the moment when Jesus arrives again. When Jesus descends to earth, the Bible suggests that both dead and living Christians will go to meet him in the air and escort him back into the world.

Since the beginning God has wanted to live among his people—and it will finally take place at the second coming of Christ.

The Final Judgment

When Jesus arrives on earth to set up his physical kingdom, he will go through a time of judgment for Christians and non-Christians alike. We have seen times of judgment all throughout biblical history—such as Noah and the flood, the Tower of Babel, Pharaoh and the plagues of Egypt, and even Israel being punished through the Babylonian exile. God is just in all he does, and we have witnessed him judging the unfaithful time and again.

At the final judgment, Jesus will give people what they deserve.

The final judgment will begin with the believers: you and I and everyone we know who has given their life to Jesus. This judgment of us will be fully public for all to see. But the judgment of believers will be different from that of non-Christians.

This time of judgment won't be about punishment for what we did on earth. It will actually be a time of reward. This will be a time of excitement and great joy for us as Christians.

Were we faithful with our calling?

Did we represent Christ well to our neighbors?

Did we spread the kingdom of God or the kingdom of the world?

What kind of fruit did our lives produce?

Our "works" don't provide us with salvation, but John wrote that our witness will be taken into account at the final judgment. And vice versa: If we have been disobedient and lived for ourselves on earth, even if we are saved, we will lose out on certain rewards. At this judgment, our true identities in Christ will be made known.

While believers are being rewarded for their good deeds and faithfulness, another far more gut-wrenching judgment will be taking place, known as the great white throne judgment. Then and there, Jesus will judge the wicked for all of their evil, dealing with them once and for all. Not only the "wicked" as we think of them, but also anyone who rejected the salvation of Jesus and partnered with the world instead of God. They've chosen to live life without God, so the great white throne judgment will give them what they've asked for.

If a person doesn't accept the free gift of salvation, they will not be covered by Jesus at this time. As Paul wrote to the Romans, "For the wages of sin is death, but the gift of God is eternal life in Christ Jesus our Lord" (Romans 6:23). No matter how good of a person they were, if they don't have Jesus, they will be judged for their sins at this point—and the wages of sin is death. They will be fully separated from God's presence for the rest of eternity in hell.

We are all given a choice in life: to partner with God or to partner with the evil forces leading the world. Our choice fully determines what happens during this time of judgment. Will we be brought into the new heaven and new earth? Or will we be cast to hell?

Hell

Isn't it interesting how so many people believe in heaven, but hell is much more taboo?

Trust me. I don't want to believe in hell any more than anyone else does. But if we believe the Bible is the living Word of God, and if we believe Scripture is telling the truth, then hell is a serious part of life.

Actually, you might have already experienced tragedies in life that you would claim to be "hell on earth."

Maybe you were abused as a child or cheated on after twenty years of marriage.

Maybe you're experiencing the painful impact of war or don't know where your next meal is coming from.

Maybe you've been dealing with an addiction that is about to take your life or grew up watching your dad physically harming your mom.

There is so much pain and suffering all around us that it sure feels like hell right now.

But the truth of the matter is that hell is far worse than anything we can experience on earth. Hell is eternal separation from God.

Did that land?

Eternal.

Separation.

From God.

The Bible describes it as a lake of fire, a bottomless pit, outer darkness, weeping, gnashing of teeth, eternal punishment, a place of suffering and torment, separation from God. Hell is a terrifying, horrible, excruciating place that nobody should want to experience. It was originally created for the devil and his demons, but all who have rejected the salvation of Jesus will also be thrown there at the end of time.

This isn't about an eternal party or a funny-looking figure with a pitchfork. Hell is a place of eternal torment and shame. It's a devastating outcome for those who went against God's will on earth and chose their sin above all.

So then we come to the question, How can a good God send someone to hell for eternity?

Because it's a great question, it has been debated for thousands of years. Since the beginning, God gave humans a choice. He wasn't a puppet master who made his creation do and say whatever he wanted them to do and say. No, God gave Adam and Eve a will and a choice to either obey his commands or do things on their own. Adam and Eve chose the devil's way, introducing sin and death into the world and separating God from humans.

The Bible also tells us that God is holy and just. He's so holy that anything sinful cannot come in contact with him. Yes, he is loving and merciful, but he hates sin with a passion because sin pulls us away from him.

So what did God do? He gave the Israelites the sacrificial system as a means of covering their sin and redeeming their relationship with him. But each sacrifice only provided a Band-Aid for their sin. It wasn't everlasting. There had to be another way to pay for our sin.

So God, out of his love for us, sent his Son, Jesus, into the world to be sacrificed once and for all as the perfect human. His death covered our sins completely, as he paid our debt on the cross. Now, if you accept Jesus' sacrifice as your own, when the Father looks at you, he sees Jesus instead. Your debt was paid. You are now holy and righteous and free from judgment.

God is full of mercy and grace. He doesn't want anyone to go to hell. He wants every single person in the world to repent and find their hope in Jesus Christ. But with that freedom comes a choice. Not everybody will make the right choice. There will always be people who reject him.

And if we believe that God is holy and just and worthy of praise, we also must believe that he will deal with the evil of the world. If the new heaven and new earth are full of peace and justice and joy and holiness, anything guided by the forces of evil can't exist in the same place. This is where hell comes into the story—as the place where people will be separated from God for all of eternity.

We have a choice: life or death. New heaven and new earth or hell.

This isn't about being scared into heaven or repeating a prayer so that one day you'll be saved from the torment of hell. It's so much bigger than that. Putting your faith in Jesus is about participating in the kingdom of God now, on earth, in preparation for the future when Jesus will reign supreme. We are to live our lives based on redemption and renewal of the world as we see it, and to live this out every day, here and now, anticipating an eternal future.

In the next chapter we'll dig into the final act: the new heaven and new earth.

One-Sentence Recap

At the second coming of Jesus, we will all be judged, leading us to either heaven or hell.

How to Apply This Lesson to Your Life

For some reason, many Christians are afraid to study hell or discuss it with their friends. On the other side of the coin, we see street corner preachers condemning people to hell. What is the appropriate way to approach it? Hell shouldn't be used as a scare tactic but rather discussed as the real outcome of living in sin and opposing the will of God. We should share the salvation message, knowing that hell will be the reality for many people.

Chapter 39

New Heaven and New Earth

Revelation 21–22

When you think of heaven, what do you envision?

A place far away in the clouds, where we float around like angels?

Where we each have a mansion and the streets are paved in gold?

A place where everyone smiles all the time, and we nod our heads to the rhythm of angels playing harps?

Did you know that's not what the Bible teaches about heaven—like, at all?

The phrase "going up to heaven" is never actually mentioned in the Bible. The authors of the Bible didn't think about the afterlife that way.

Some people still have this gnostic idea that everything here on this physical earth is bad while everything spiritual must be good. In this worldview, the spiritual world and the physical world are two completely separate things. So if things on the physical earth are "bad," then heaven must not be a physical place at all. The same people usually believe that at the end of time, we're going to leave this world behind and make our eternal home in a faraway heaven, up in the metaphorical clouds or maybe in some other dimension altogether. These people say they're "just passing through" earth until a later date. This sort of mentality can be incredibly damaging because it totally disregards God's original plan.

God didn't make a mistake. His original plan is still the plan.

So what was the plan? Well, in order to understand where we are going, we need to look back at where we started: in the garden of Eden.

Promise of a New Creation

According to the biblical authors, there were two separate "dimensions," if you will: heaven (the place God occupied) and earth (where humans resided). Some may think heaven is completely spiritual and earth is completely physical, but that's not how they understood things.

In the beginning, heaven and earth were essentially overlapping in the garden of Eden. God's space was joined with human space. God could walk freely among his people because no sin existed to mess with God's holiness. Adam and Eve were partners alongside God to work the land, procreate, and expand the garden.

That is, until the fall took place—when Adam and Eve ate from the forbidden Tree of Knowledge of Good and Evil and separated the heavenly realm from the earthly realm. Since God refuses to interact with sin, he split the two spaces, kicking the humans out of the garden so they wouldn't remain in their sinful state for the rest of eternity.

Later, you'll remember, God commanded Moses to build the tabernacle and Solomon to build the temple. Both were supposed to be places for God to call "home" on earth. The Hebrews saw these places as the locations where heaven and earth overlapped once again. The tabernacle was full of garden of Eden imagery—fruit trees, angels, flowers, etc.—so that when people visited the temple, they felt as if they were being transported back to the garden.

It was heavenly for them.

Within the temple was the holy of holies—the place where the ark of the covenant was and where God's presence lived. This was the most holy place in all of the world.

But the temple could only be in one location, and God wanted to fill the entire earth.

So God sent Jesus to earth to take on the sin of those who put their faith in him. Everywhere Jesus went, he brought heaven to that location.

All throughout Galilee and Judea, with Samaritans and Jews and Gentiles alike, heaven and earth collided in a way that people could have never imagined. It seemed as if the two dimensions were slowly merging back together. Jesus even taught his followers to pray to God: "Your kingdom come. Your will be done on earth as it is in heaven" (Matthew 6:10).

Heaven was invading earth.

After Jesus was crucified and resurrected, he was the "firstfruit" of the new creation. Nobody had ever risen from the dead like that before. Yes, a few stories in Scripture spoke of people rising from the dead, but never in a glorified body. Jesus was the first of a new kind of person.

Things were different now.

As the first to be resurrected and the prototype for a new creation, Jesus gave us an image for what was to come. He also gave us a role in spreading heaven, in overlapping heaven and earth everywhere we go.

This whole plan was launched through Jesus and will one day come to fruition through Jesus. It's all about Jesus. And Jesus is currently in heaven on the throne, in his resurrected body, not in his spiritual, disembodied state. Jesus is in human form. Right now. In heaven. Let that sink in.

So how can we bring heaven to earth in our day-to-day? Well, that's why God sent the Holy Spirit: to connect heaven and earth through us, a place where the two realms are joined together again. As you and I spread the kingdom of God throughout our day, we get one inch closer to heaven and earth merging. We have a role to play! We can't just sit back waiting for all of this to end so we get "transported to heaven." Our job is to help bring heaven to the here and now.

We are spreading this new creation, the kingdom of God, which Jesus initiated through every one of our actions and decisions. Every time we choose to obey God, we get closer and closer.

Because Jesus was the first of the new creation, of the resurrected body, we have hope that one day we, too, will be in our glorified bodies—free from pain, disease, depression, injury; glorified in ways we can't even begin to imagine.

The Bible story is a story of how God will bring both "dimensions" back together again, once and for all. He still wants to dwell among his people for all eternity. The plan has never changed. There have just been a few speed bumps along the way.

The New Heaven and New Earth

At the end of Revelation, as John wrote to the churches who dealt with loads of persecution and felt like their world was falling apart, he gave them a sense of hope, a promise for the future. And this hope was rooted in the belief that Jesus had come to save them from the punishment of sin and was in the process of making all things new.

John described a city coming down from heaven, called the New Jerusalem. Heaven and earth were finally being joined together. John's readers had been waiting for this image. They were going back to the garden, but John described the new Jerusalem as more of an advanced version—a city for living and playing and working the land in physically glorified bodies, just as Adam and Eve were once called to do.

God is redeeming, renewing, restoring, repairing creation back to its original intent. This time, however, God is removing all sin and death so we can remain in peace and harmony for all of eternity, surrounded by God's presence. God's glory will fill the entire world, making it all the holy of holies.

This is what we put our faith in as Christians: not that we will turn into ghosts or angels and float away from this place playing harps in our little white bathrobes but that Jesus is coming back to earth, transforming it into a new heaven and new earth. The Bible says we will be corulers, creating something remarkable together. God dwelling among his people in harmony, with no corrupting influence from the Evil One. He has been dealt with for the rest of eternity, as we saw in the last chapter.

So what will life be like in the new heaven and new earth?

Well, for starters, there will be no more tears or pain, sin or death, corruption or shame. All of that will be removed for the rest of eternity. That alone is mind-blowing.

We can only begin to imagine what it will be like. It will be a million times more amazing than we can comprehend. Like the beauty and goodness of all creation is at its full potential. We will be in harmony with God.

We need to understand that the whole world, everything, is negatively impacted by sin right now.

Everything.

Trees don't look the way they should.

We don't look the way we should.

Fruit doesn't taste the way it should.

Our desires aren't the way they should be.

But in this new, restored creation, all things will have been made new. Nature flourishing, fruit succulent, humans thriving in community with one another.

Just as Adam and Eve were told to cultivate the earth—told to help bring creation into its full potential—we, too, will have a job to do, but in the most meaningful and fulfilling way. Our work won't be a slog or full of difficult, boring, or repetitive labor. It will be meaningful and fulfilling.

We'll have good food and good music, art and creativity, the pursuit of passions and sports if you're into that, all in worship to our Creator. And we'll have it forever. The word *forever* sounds scary now, but that's just because of our limited ability to understand eternity from our fallen perspective. Experiencing eternity won't be frightening. It'll feel the way it was always supposed to feel.

Joy and laughter.

Dancing and smiles.

Purpose and fulfillment.

A place where we will enjoy the best of the best, all out of God's abundant love for us.

My words could never do it justice, but I'll never stop trying despite knowing eternity will be far greater than I could imagine. As followers of Jesus, believing he was resurrected from the dead, we can have hope for a future when the rest of creation, including us, will be perfected and made new. This is where we put our hope, no matter what comes our way in life. We are to live in that anticipation, as citizens of God's kingdom right now. That's something to get excited about.

One-Sentence Recap

The biblical hope for the future doesn't describe heaven as a place far away in the clouds, but as a fully redeemed, restored, renewed world right here, where heaven and earth will one day overlap again.

How to Apply This Lesson to Your Life

As Christians, our role is to spread heaven into every area of our influence. We have hope for the future when God's plan will be complete, but until that day comes, we can do our parts now.

Part Ten

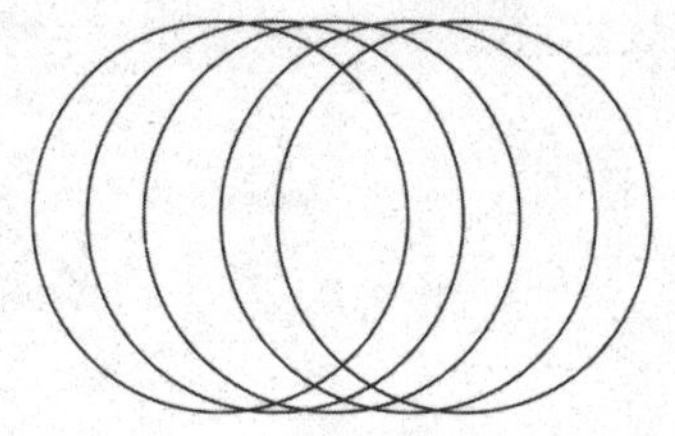

HOW TO BE A CHRISTIAN

Chapter 40

Living Out Your Faith

Understanding the entire Bible story and being "saved" are only the first steps of our journey as followers of Jesus. It all becomes real and tangible when we allow our faith to impact the way we live and treat those around us. Viewing life in light of eternity ought to do something inside of us; we are no longer the same people we once were.

You are now part of this renewal project God is doing on earth, powered by his Spirit. We have a role to play. And Jesus is asking, *Will you join me?* When you understand that role, your life will never be the same. You have been born again. You are a new creation. God wants to partner with you to change his world. That's a big deal!

When you begin to view life from an eternal perspective, you can live with purpose in the "now." Every single thing you do with your life impacts whether the kingdom of God comes to life around you. Every time you obey God, the kingdom is expanded. That's not something to be taken lightly. This should impact every decision you make, with the kingdom in mind.

Everything you do in life matters. Nothing is wasted.

Our lives should be reflections of heaven in our stances, our treatment of others, our work ethic, our attitude, the music we listen to, and the art we create. And as the world sees God's goodness, the gospel message of what Jesus is up to will make a whole lot more sense.

And how do we do that? How do we dedicate ourselves to building the kingdom and embodying that reality in the present world?

We live out the three main Christian virtues of faith, hope, and love.

Faith

Faith is an action, not a mindset.

Faith isn't just about believing in Jesus or having faith in God. True faith that is acted out is consumed by trusting in God. Hebrews 11:1 says, "Faith is confidence in what we hope for and assurance about what we do not see" (NIV). Living out your faith means trusting in God, even when it doesn't make sense.

Have you ever been in a situation where you say to yourself, *God, I don't know what you're up to, but I trust that you're working it out for good*? That's what it means to live out your faith. When you can't see a positive ending but remain faithful, trusting that God's plan is greater than yours, you're living in faith.

Faith is when you focus on God's will over your own, being obedient to what you've been called to even when you'd do things differently.

True faith is seen in your prayer life when things get tough. It's seen in your confidence when God calls you to step out and follow the plan and purpose that has been placed on your life. It's seen in the way you interact with your friends and family members and coworkers who are also going through challenges.

Once you truly trust God, the way you live should never be the same. This may not be easy at first though. Think of your faith like a muscle. At first it's weak, and you're going to make a lot of mistakes. But as time goes on and you live out your faith more and more, it will become easier for you. Soon you will feel confident that God is going to do even greater things in your life.

How do we grow in our faith?

First, we become a disciple of Jesus. Just as Jesus went up to the disciples and told them to follow him as their rabbi, he does the same thing for us today. He wants you and me to be his disciples, to learn from him, to study under him, and to do what he did. As followers of Jesus, we should learn to imitate him in all we do.

This begins by immersing yourself in Scripture, prayer, and worship—building "holy habits" into your routine that encourage you to grow closer to God. If you want to learn to imitate Jesus, you need to understand who he is, what he did, and how he asks us to live.

Second, we learn to have more faith by just beginning. The more we do, the more we grow closer to God—so if we practice having faith in the small areas of life, one day we will have faith for the really big stuff. Nobody expects you to master everything right away. Just take the first step and trust that God will guide you in all the steps to come.

And third, whether good or bad, the people you surround yourself with are going to rub off on you. So another way to grow in faith is to surround yourself with people who are further along in their faith than you. Get involved at your church, make some Christian friends, join a discipleship group or a class, and listen to the testimonies of how God has moved in others' lives. The more stories you hear of God coming through, the more your faith will be boosted. Then you will begin to expect miracles in your life as well.

Learning how to grow in faith can be life-changing. So if you want to spread the kingdom of God here on earth, start with your faith.

Hope

The second Christian virtue that should be rooted in who we are is hope. For us Christians, hope isn't just about being optimistic when our circumstances say otherwise. Hope is our confidence in God's character and knowing that the work Jesus did on the cross was only the beginning. He is coming back with power to transform the entire world into his kingdom.

Our hope is in our present mindset.
Our hope is our confidence in his return.
Our hope roots us in purpose.
Our hope is that what Jesus said is actually true.
Our hope is that the new heaven and new earth are on the way.

Romans 15:13 says, "May the God of hope fill you with all joy and peace as you believe so that you may overflow with hope by the power of the Holy Spirit."

Since we have hope for the future, our everyday lives can now be saturated in purpose and the desire to live righteously in the ways of God. We believe Jesus rose from the dead and began the new creation, and we are called to participate in it *now*, not in the future. That's our hope. That should change the way we live. We should be lights to the world in all we do, showing our neighbors that there is so much more to live for. When they are going through hard times, we can be a positive voice in their lives because we know another way. When Satan tries to tear them down mentally and physically, we have the power of the Holy Spirit inside of us to show them the truth.

That's where our hope is rooted.

So how do we remain tangibly full of hope?

First, we remain focused on eternity, remembering that Jesus is coming back to renew and restore the earth. The new heaven and new earth is our eternal destiny where all pain, sadness, and hardship will be completely removed. When we learn to view life through the lens of God, with an eternal perspective, our mindset shifts to the present even though we are focusing on the future.

Next, Colossians 3:1–2 says, "If you're serious about living this new resurrection life with Christ, act like it. Pursue the things over which Christ presides. Don't shuffle along, eyes to the ground, absorbed with the things right in front of you. Look up, and be alert to what is going on around Christ—that's where the action is. See things from his perspective" (MSG).

When we learn to focus on the good and the places where God is moving, the goodness around us gets bigger and bigger. And the opposite is also true: When we focus solely on the bad and where the Enemy is moving in our lives, the bad things grow. I don't know about you, but I want to live a life full of God's goodness and hope. To do so makes life so much more enjoyable, and I want that for you too.

Learning to focus on the good comes from having a big-picture perspective of where God's story is headed.

Love

The final Christian virtue we should learn to live out is love. Love is central to God's character and should be the foundation of our actions. Jesus said the greatest commandment is to "Love the Lord your God with all your heart, with all your soul, and with all your mind." Then he said the second greatest command is just like it: to "Love your neighbor as yourself" (Matthew 22:37, 39).

Love is far more than a nice feeling. Loving your neighbor is a commitment to getting to know them—focusing on the best for those around us through grace, forgiveness, seeking justice and mercy, acts of kindness, service to others, and generosity. Love isn't first and foremost about how we "feel" about someone else. We need to love even when we don't feel like it. We even need to love the people we don't really like.

Thomas Merton wrote, "Love seeks one thing only: the good of the one loved. It leaves all the other secondary effects to take care of themselves. Love, therefore, is its own reward."[1] True, Christian love is based upon looking at the other person and actually caring for their best interest. That can be hard to do sometimes, can't it? But it's necessary in the kingdom.

When we love others with our actions, we reflect the heart of God to our communities. Jesus said, "By this everyone will know that you are my disciples, if you love one another" (John 13:35).

Is that true for you?

Do people look at the way you love others and know you are a disciple of Jesus because of it?

That should be the goal for each of us. It's easy to say we believe in Jesus and follow the Bible, but do we actually? Have we taken the intellectual head knowledge of the gospel message and moved it to our hearts and hands and feet?

If you don't know where to start, start here: Jesus told us to share the good news, feed the hungry, give drinks to the thirsty, be hospitable to strangers, clothe the naked, look after the sick, and visit those in prison. There are seven things right there. As you can see, Jesus has a real heart for the people our society is bad at loving—people like the poor, the homeless, the strangers, and the incarcerated. As Christians, we reflect Jesus when we love people who tend to be lower in society's superficial ranks.

God wants to love the world through us. And loving others is the heartbeat of the new creation. This kind of love transforms the world. We have a responsibility to be the good in the world, not just to live in a bubble hoping we don't get any sin on us, waiting for the day when we eventually leave this place.

No, Jesus calls us to start with simple actions that build up over time. You don't need to go and start an orphanage (by all means, do so if God puts it on your heart—that would be amazing!), but you can start small within your daily interactions. This comes back to viewing the world from God's perspective instead of our own. God wants to use you, and everywhere you look there are opportunities to show others the love of Christ. Try to do one small thing every day. If you miss a day, that's okay. Start back up tomorrow, and over time your small actions will contribute to much larger ones.

Begin by looking at your friends, family, and coworkers. How can you show them the love of God? How can you bring heaven into your interactions? That will be up to you to decide because each situation is different. But you can open your eyes and simply make yourself available to others. You'd be surprised how impactful lending a listening ear can be.

Do one thing for Jesus today. Send an encouraging text, buy a meal for someone, ask how your friends are really doing, pray for someone's healing, donate money to an organization, stand up for injustice—one small thing every day can snowball into so much more for someone else.

God is inviting us to participate in his story of renewal, and three of the greatest ways to embody the kingdom in the present world are through faith, hope, and love.

We have faith to trust that God is in control, we have hope that he is coming back, and we have a task to love every person we encounter until then, even when it's difficult. So start small and start today. And as you grow in anticipation of Jesus' second coming, I believe those around you will begin to know you're a follower of Jesus through your actions above all.

Final Thoughts

When you first opened this book, you most likely thought it was going to be a simple layout of the Bible that you'd expect to receive at Sunday school—but my hope and prayer is that it was so much more than that for you. This was a deep dive into the Bible like most people have never experienced. You now know the biblical story better than a lot of your friends and family members and even people at your church. That's pretty cool.

So congratulations on growing in your relationship with God and becoming more confident in the Bible.

Just as the rabbis would place honey on their students' slates on the first day of Torah school, I pray that the words of this book have been honey to your life—that you've tasted and seen that God is good.

But now the process continues.

Now that you've read this book, it's time to do the real work. It's time to study the Bible for the rest of your life—actually reading it and digesting it.

Charles Spurgeon once said, "Nobody ever outgrows Scripture; the book widens and deepens with our years."[1]

The Bible is a living, breathing book that will teach you something new every time you open it. You will be able to study it for the rest of your life and still never fully understand it all. That shouldn't overwhelm you but excite you—that the God we serve is far bigger than we could ever imagine.

For your next steps, flip to the recommended resources on the next page. This is just the beginning, but your path has been laid.

If this book has been a blessing to you and you've learned a lot, I hope you will pass it along to three friends or family members who might also benefit from learning the Bible.

Thank you for reading. I'm honored that you chose this book. If we don't meet on this side of heaven, I hope we get to later on.

Zach

Recommended Resources for Further Study

I owe everything in this book to my time studying the brilliant theologians and teachers we have access to today. People like N. T. Wright, Dwight A. Pryor, John Walton, Timothy Keller, David A. deSilva, F. F. Bruce, Leon L. Morris, T. Desmond Alexander, Walter Brueggemann, Wayne Grudem, Craig S. Keener, R. T. France, G. K. Beale, Ben Witherington III, Scot McKnight, Tim Mackie, TheosU, Alfred Edersheim, David Pawson, Kenneth Bailey, Ray Vander Laan, Dallas Willard, Randy Alcorn, and many, many others.

If you are continuing your Bible journey but are just starting out, I recommend purchasing a nice leather Bible, a Bible dictionary, and a commentary. You have thousands of options to choose from at all sorts of price points, so it's really up to you which direction to go.

Here is a basic list to start with:

- *The Bible Study* by Zach Windahl
- *Holman Illustrated Bible Dictionary* by Chad Brand
- *New Bible Commentary* by Gordon J. Wenham

- *A Survey of the Old Testament* by Andrew E. Hill and John H. Walton
- *The New Testament in Its World* by N. T. Wright and Michael F. Bird

If you want a more in-depth Bible dictionary, the one I use most often is *The Anchor Bible Dictionary* (a six-book set).

If you want my other most commonly referenced commentaries:

- *HarperCollins Bible Commentary*, edited by James L. Mays
- *The New Interpreters Bible Commentary* (a ten-volume set)
- *IVP Bible Background Commentary* (both volumes)
- *The New American Commentary* (a multivolume series)
- *Tyndale New Testament Commentaries* (a twenty-volume set)
- *Pillar New Testament Commentary* (a seventeen-volume series)
- *The JPS Torah Commentary* (a five-volume series)
- *New International Commentary on the New Testament* (a forty-six-volume set)

If you prefer digital instead of print, download Logos Bible Software. From there you can buy nearly every commentary and dictionary available. It's a gold mine.

If you are looking for other books about the Bible:

- *30 Days to Understanding the Bible* by Max Anders
- *Read the Bible for a Change* by Ray Lubeck
- *How to Read the Bible for All Its Worth* by Gordon Fee and Douglas Stuart
- *The Epic of Eden* by Sandra L. Richter

Finally, read everything by N. T. Wright. Start with *Simply Jesus*, *Simply Christian*, and *Surprised by Hope*. Prepare to have your mind blown, in the best way possible.

Acknowledgments

As I sit here writing the last few pages of this book, I'm overwhelmed with gratitude. I didn't think I would ever write another book; my attention was going in a different direction from the publishing space. But God had a different plan.

Writing this book changed my life. It pushed me. It molded me. It made me fall more in love with Scripture than ever before.

I couldn't have done any of this on my own. Writing a book takes a team of people who spend countless hours perfecting every little detail to bring it to life in this way.

For starters, I want to thank my wife, Gisela, for being the greatest influence on this book coming to completion. You are incredibly wise, tuned in to the Holy Spirit, and patient. I love you. And I can't wait to begin raising our son together in a few short weeks.

Thank you to Andrew Stoddard, Daniel Marrs, Hanha Parham, Kathryn Duke, and the entire team at Nelson Books. Thank you for working tirelessly on this project and being willing to take some risks. You are all such a pleasure to work alongside.

Thank you to my literary agent, Esther Fedorkevich, for believing in this project before anyone else did and putting all the pieces in place to make it happen.

Thank you to my cover designer, Kary Acevedo. You are a master of your craft. I'm always inspired by the attention to detail and focus on excellence that you bring to a project. This one turned out beautifully.

Thank you to my friends Matt Velasco and Will Degraw for reading the earliest version of the manuscript in order to poke holes in it, only to make it better.

Thank you to my Bible study group—Dylan, Kerem, Ricky, Yoly, Derick, Justin, Tammi, Arman, Alexis, Austin, Vanessa, Daniella, Luis, and Katie—who allowed me to flesh out ideas without even knowing it.

Thank you to my parents and in-laws—Pete, T, Tony, and Elsa—for teaching me more about Jesus every day through your words and actions. Te amo.

Notes

Introduction

1. A. W. Tozer, *The Quotable Tozer*, ed. James L. Snyder (Bethany House, 2018), 36.

Chapter 1: What Is the Bible?

1. For more on this, check out *Reading the Bible for a Change: Understanding and Responding to God's Word* by Ray Lubeck (Wipf and Stock, 2023).
2. Carsten Peter Thiede, "367 Athanasius Defines the New Testament," *Christian History Magazine* (1990), 10–11, https://christianhistoryinstitute.org/magazine/issue/100-most-important-events-in-church-history.
3. *Britannica*, "Vulgate," last updated January 22, 2025, https://www.britannica.com/topic/Vulgate.

Chapter 2: How to Read the Bible

1. For more on this, check out the chapter "Greek Brain, Hebrew Brain" in Lois Tverberg's book *Reading the Bible with Rabbi Jesus: How a Jewish Perspective Can Transform Your Understanding* (Baker Books, 2017).

Chapter 4: Creation and the Fall

1. Brown-Driver-Briggs, "Chata," in *The New American Standard Old Testament Hebrew Lexicon*, Bible Study Tools, accessed January 9, 2025, https://www.biblestudytools.com/lexicons/hebrew/nas/chata.html.

Chapter 5: Cain and Abel

1. Nahum M. Sarna et al., *Genesis*, JPS Torah Commentary (Jewish Publication Society, 1989), 39.

Chapter 7: The Tower of Babel

1. From book 1, chapter 4 of *Antiquities of the Jews* in Flavius Josephus, *Josephus: Complete Works*, trans. William Whiston (Kregel Publications, 1960), 30.
2. Nahum M. Sarna et al., *Genesis*, JPS Torah Commentary (Jewish Publication Society, 1989), 84.

Chapter 11: The Early Life of Moses

1. Nahum M. Sarna et al., *Exodus*, JPS Torah Commentary (Jewish Publication Society, 1991), 9.
2. Sarna et al., *Exodus*, 9.

Chapter 30: The Final Week

1. Flavius Josephus, *Josephus: Complete Works*, trans. William Whiston (Kregel Publications, 1960), 588.
2. *Path to the Cross*, volume 11, "The Last Supper," hosted by Ray Vanderlaan, directed by Bob Garner (That the World May Know, 1992), https://www.thattheworldmayknow.com/the-path-to-the-cross.

Chapter 31: Trial and Crucifixion

1. William Barclay, *The Gospel of John*, vol. 2, rev. ed. (Westminster John Knox Press, 1975), 221.
2. N. T. Wright and Michael F. Bird, *The New Testament in Its World* (Zondervan Academic, 2019), 242.

Chapter 40: Living Out Your Faith

1. Thomas Merton, *No Man Is an Island* (Shambhala Publications, 2005), 3.

Final Thoughts

1. Charles H. Spurgeon, "The Talking Book," sermon, Metropolitan Tabernacle in London, UK, October 22, 1871, transcript, *Spurgeon's Sermons*, vol. 17, *1871*, archived at Christian Classics Ethereal Library, https://ccel.org/ccel/spurgeon/sermons17/sermons17.l.html.

Photo Credits

Page 24: iStock.com/duncan1890.
Page 82: iStock.com/ZU_09.
Page 83: iStock.com/ZU_09.
Page 108: iStock.com/ZU_09.
Page 164: iStock.com/THEPALMER.
Page 198: iStock.com/cjp.
Page 230: iStock.com/bauhaus1000.

About the Author

Zach Windahl is an author and content creator focused on helping people grow in their faith. He is the author of several books, including *The Bible Study: A One-Year Study of the Bible and How It Relates to You.* He lives in Orlando, Florida, with his wife, Gisela. You can connect with Zach on social media at @ZachWindahl or at www.ZachWindahl.com.